OUR EYES CAN BE OPENED

P9-CFV-779

Preaching the Miracle
Stories of the
Synoptic Gospels Today

Ronald J. Allen

UNIVERSITY
PRESS OF
AMERICA

LANHAM • NEW YORK • LONDON

Copyright © 1982 by

University Press of America,™ Inc.

4720 Boston Way
Lanham, MD 20706

3 Henrietta Street
London WC2E 8LU England

Library of Congress Cataloging in
Publication Data

Allen, Ronald J.
    Our eyes can be opened.

    Bibliography: p.
    1. Jesus Christ--Miracles. 2.
Preaching. I. Title.
BT366.A44   1982   226'.706   81-43679
ISBN 0-8191-2671-3 (pbk.: Alk. paper)

To

.Linda McKiernan-Allen

Spouse

Colleague

Friend

The Mother of our Son

Lover

Heir of the Promise

Together we dream, break bread and lie down

ACKNOWLEDGEMENTS

Grateful acknowledgement is made for permission to
quote from the following:

Theological Dictionary of the New Testament, ed. G.
Kittel and G. Friedrich, by permission of Wm. B. Eerdmans, publisher.

Documents from Old Testament Times by D.W. Thomas by
permission of Thomas Nelson and Sons, Ltd. and Harper
and Row, British and American publishers respectively.

"Death, Theology of," by W. Brueggemann, The Interpreter's Dictionary of the Bible, Supplementary Volume,
by permission of Abingdon Press, publisher.

Language and Myth by E. Cassirer, tr. S.K. Langer by
permission of Dover Publications, publisher.

"The Primary Illusions and the Great Orders of Art" by
S.K. Langer, reprinted by permission from The Hudson
Review, Vol. III, No. 2 (Summer 1950). Copyright ©
1950 by The Hudson Review, Inc.

An Essay on Man by E. Cassirer by permission of Yale
University Press, publisher.

The Philosophy of Symbolic Forms, 3 vols., by E. Cassirer, tr. R. Manheim, by permission of Yale University
Press, publisher.

From Tradition to Gospel by M. Dibelius, tr. B. Woolf
(New York: Charles Scribner's Sons, 1935). Reprinted
with the permission of Charles Scribner's Sons.

Feeling and Form: A Theory of Art Developed from Philosophy in a New Key, by S.K. Langer. Copyright 1953
Charles Scribner's Sons; copyright renewed 1981 Susanne K. Langer (New York; Charles Scribner's Sons,
1953). Reprinted with the permission of Charles
Scribner's Sons.

TABLE OF CONTENTS

PREFACE

Like a beehive, the miracle stories of the synoptic gospels are both attractive and unsettling. On the one hand, we are drawn to the wholeness and power which they picture. On the other hand, we are sometimes unsettled, and even embarrassed, by them. As a consequence many of us are not quite sure what to make of them as we step into the pulpit on Sunday morning. We are drawn to the honeycomb but unsettled by the bees.

It is important to distinguish between the actual event of the miracle and the miracle stories.[1] I am not concerned with miraculous events as such. Instead, I am interested in the miracle stories.

Recent investigation into the nature of narrative suggests that the meaning of a story is often in the story itself. Details are sensitively interwoven to create the rich fabric of the whole narrative. I interpret selected miracle stories of the synoptic tradition as stories. Because a story is rooted in the realities of a particular era, I attempt to recall as much of the ancient cultural, theological, mythical aesthetic and historical background as may facilitate our understanding of the stories for preaching. Indeed the preaching ministry is the intended audience of the work.

Critical interpretation of the New Testament allows us to distinguish three levels of tradition within many of the texts of the first three gospels: (1) The setting of the text in the life and ministry of Jesus and the disciples; (2) The use of the text in the period of oral tradition; (3) The placement and creative formulation and use of the text in its present context in the gospel. The redactors, whom we know by the names of Matthew, Mark and Luke, have often artfully shaped and placed miracle stories (like all texts) to serve their particular theological and polemical purposes. The focus of this work, however, is a neglected aspect of the life of the miracle stories in the period of oral tradition.

This brief work is not intended to supplant other
examinations of the miracle stories. Rather, it is a
supplement. Those who seek a comprehensive history of
the development of the miracle traditions must look
elsewhere. The questions of the Biblical guild which
are crucial for the history and character of early
Christianity but which do not, at the present time,
seem to me to press their special claim on the
preaching ministry have been left unattended. I have
tried to be representative, but not exhaustive, in conversation with the immense secondary literature. Further, I have not tried to duplicate information
readily available in the commentaries. This work
needs to be used in concert with resources for Biblical interpretation which will be found on a thoughtful
pastor's shelf.

Cursory attention is given to the use of the
miracle stories by Matthew, Mark and Luke. Even the
uninitiated reader will see that these discussions are
not thorough analyses. Where interpretive consensus
has been established, I generally report or modify
that consensus. While I have not been afraid to present other conclusions when the text seems to call
for them, this has not seemed the place to undertake
complete redaction-critical inquiries.

In each of the exegetical chapters (III-VIII), I
recall a rough form of the text as it may have circulated in the oral tradition. Even when tediously done
and accompanied by the bold assertions of scholars,
such reconstruction is always tentative.

I join the chorus of scholars in thinking that
Mark's texts of the miracle stories are often closer
to the oral tradition than those of Matthew or Luke.
Each text must be evaluated individually, of course,
and sensitive application of redaction-critical and
form-critical procedures can yield an earlier version.
Because of widespread agreement that Mark assumes an
apocalyptic milieu characterized by conflict between
God and Satan, a difficult problem has been the decision as to which layer of tradition to assign those
aspects of the text which depict the miracle as a
struggle between God and Satan, sometimes in the language of exorcism. Do such elements belong to Mark or
do they rise from the earlier tradition? Lacking convincing alternatives, I have assigned those elements
which are not obviously Markan to the oral tradition.

Each of the exegetical chapters concludes with a section entitled, "The Use of the Story in Preaching." Those remarks, like the sermons in chapter IX, derive from the study of the story as story in the second level of development. The comments are intended to open windows for the interpretive imagination. I will be happy if the flint of the studies strikes a different spark against the steel of the preacher.

In the first chapter, I quickly survey and critique several leading approaches to the miracle stories. In making critical judgments about other interpretations, I do not mean to be cavalier or disrespectful, nor do I mean to imply that other approaches have no significant light to shed. I hope the effect of the chapter is to help the reader realize that no one approach to the miracle stories can account for their richness and vitality.

I am indebted to my teachers at The Graduate School of Drew University where the seeds of this work were sown: Charles Rice, Neill Hamilton, Darrell Doughty, Kalyan Dey. My interest in the inter-relationship between Biblical studies and preaching was earlier awakened by Edmund Steimle, J. Louis Martyn and Walter Wink of Union Theological Seminary, New York. James Crouch, Robert Simpson and Gary Midkiff provided introduction to the historical-critical method and Shelden Shirts first put the Greek New Testament in my hands. My friend Larry Bowden read parts of the manuscript at an earlier stage and offered editorial and substantive suggestions.

The work is dedicated to Linda McKiernan-Allen who gave me the year in which to work.

Though this cloud of witnesses will not all agree on the thrust of the project, perhaps it can be accepted as a small way of saying, "Thank you."

Ronald J. Allen
First Christian Church

Easter, 1982   Grand Island, Nebraska

NOTES

[1]H.D. Betz, "The Early Christian Miracle Story: Some Observations on the Form-Critical Problem," *Semeia* 11 (1978), p. 70.

ABBREVIATIONS

AB	Anchor Bible
Bib	Biblica
BibZ	Biblische Zeitschrift
CB	Century Bible
CBQ	Catholic Biblical Quarterly
ERE	Encyclopedia of Religion and Ethics
HNTC	Harper's New Testament Commentaries
HST	History of the Synoptic Tradition
IB	The Interpreter's Bible
IDB	The Interpreter's Dictionary of the Bible
Interp	Interpretation
JBL	Journal of Biblical Literature
JTS	Journal of Theological Studies
NIGTC	New International Greek Testament Commentary
NTS	New Testament Studies
NT	Novum Testamentum
RGG	Die Religion in Geschichte und Gegenwart
SBT	Studies in Biblical Theology
SJT	Scottish Journal of Theology
ST	Studia Theologica
TDNT	Theological Dictionary of the New Testament
TZ	Theologische Zeitschrift
ZNW	Zeitschrift fuer die Neutestamentlichen Wissenschaft

CHAPTER I

RECENT INTERPRETATION OF THE MIRACLE STORIES

A lens focuses our attention in a particular way. One lens magnifies while another realigns our line of vision. Still another accentuates some things while diminishing others. We who wear glasses notice our vision becoming distorted; perhaps our eyes have weakened or perhaps a squirt from the breakfast grapefruit has made an island in the center of a lens. When our glasses are reground or cleaned, we see with new clarity that which the lens is prepared to pick up.

Similarly, we read the miracle stories with lenses ground to our particular Biblical and theological viewpoints. I identify seven major lenses through which interpretation of the miracle stories is focused. These include the miracle stories: (1) As reports of the breach of natural law; (2) As illusions; (3) As proofs that Jesus is the Messiah; (4) As signs of the reign of God; (5) As models of ministry; (6) As models of behavior; (7) As Stories.

The lens through which one interprets the miracle stories yields homiletical emphases characteristic of that viewpoint. While the viewpoints are not always mutually exclusive, each does result in the magnification of some dimensions and the diminuation of others.[1]

1. Miracle Stories and Natural Law

The miracle stories are often seen as newspaper-like accounts of the breach of natural law. In this view, the world operates according to inviolate natural laws which are broken only by divine intervention.

Those who adopt this position marshall arguments to demonstrate the plausibility of events occuring in the way they are reported. The reliability of the Bible is at stake: if one can establish the probability that the miracles actually "happened," then one has evidence that the Bible is "true" and worthy of our belief and obedience.

Preaching on a miracle story from this perspective takes on the quality of a scientific report. The preacher accumulates evidence to show why things happened in the way described in the miracle story.

However fascinating such an approach may be, especially to those who are impressed by the scientific way of thinking, it raises significant problems.[2] In the first place, the first century world had no such concept of natural law.[3] In any case, we cannot today scientifically "prove" that the miraculous events of the past took place in just the way described.

This view is further troubled by the fact that in the gospel tradition, parallel accounts of the same miracle stories often disagree in both major and minor details. For example, how did those who brought the paralytic to Jesus get through the roof (Mt. 9:2/Mk. 2:4/Lk. 5:19)? How many people did Jesus heal outside of Jericho and how did he do it (Mt. 20:29-34/Mk. 10:46-52/Lk. 18:35-43)?

This approach makes faith in God depend upon the scientific accuracy of the Bible.[4] Ironically, this is not a Biblical view of faith.[4] Recent research also indicates that neither the traditions embedded in the gospels nor the gospels themselves are intended to be scientific reports. Rather, the traditions and the gospels are creatively shaped theological documents. The meaning of the miracle stories, then, cannot be reduced to scientific inquiry.

2. Miracles as Illusions

Some interpreters see the miraculous element in a miracle story as an illusion. Something happened long ago, but not in the way reported: the miraculous element is explained away. This line of thinking attempts to preserve a factual basis for the story while making the event seem credible to the modern scientific mind.

2

For example, the disciples, alone and afraid on the storm-tossed sea, thought Jesus was walking on the water when, in fact, he was walking on the shore. The incident was an optical illusion. When the multitude was hungry in the wilderness, many people had picnic lunches under their robes. At mealtime, at Jesus' direction, they shared their food with those who had none.

Preaching which derives from this perspective typically moves in two phases. First, the preacher "explains" the incident. Then, the preacher draws out a "lesson" which the story teachers. For example, the story of the feeding of the multitude teaches the necessity of sharing.

While fascinating, such explanations do not allow the miracle stories to be what they patently are: miracle stories. Such thinking further imposes a modern concept of science upon stories to whom such concern is foreign. The "lessons" are often quite unrelated to the subject matter of the stories. Such efforts, thus, have little significance for the life of faith.

3. Miracle Stories as Proofs

The miracles themselves (as reported) are said to prove that Jesus is the Messiah. Indeed, to some, the miracles are proof that Jesus was who he said he was: only the Son of God could work miracles. A twist to this viewpoint is that the early church is said to have used the miracle stories in its missionary preaching to persuade those outside the church that Jesus was indeed "the expected one."

Preaching from this viewpoint is much like a legal brief. Emphasis is not on proving that the miracles happened but on showing how the miracle (story) demonstrates the messiahship of Jesus. The goal of the sermon is to win (or reinforce) an affirmation that Jesus is the Messiah, and further, in some circles, to foster the belief that if Jesus could perform miracles in the ancient world then as the resurrected Lord he could certainly make miracles happen now.

However, the first century expectation of miracle working was not limited to the Messiah. Other figures such as "prophet" and "divine man" were regarded as

3

miracle workers. Reports of miraculous events similar to those recounted in the gospels and Acts are found in extra-Biblical literature from both Greek and Jewish cultures.[5] While, in the ancient world, the capacity to work miracles may have added to one's credibility as a divinely inspired person, or may have added authenticity to one's teaching,[6] reports of miracle working power were not unique to Jesus. Indeed, texts like Mark 9:38-41 and Acts 13:6 report the activity of miracle workers who were not associated with the church. Thus, even apart from the enormously complicated question of the messianic self-consciousness of Jesus, the miracles could not uniquely demonstrate messiahship.

4. Miracles as Signs

The miracles have been considered signs of the inbreaking of the reign of God. Miraculous events demonstrate in miniature what the reign of God will be like in its fullness. Additionally, they show that the power of the reign is already operative. Parts of the early church perceived the miracles as such signs and apparently used the miracle stories to call attention to the dawning reign of God (e.g. Mt. 11:2-14/Lk. 7:18-35). Emphasis is not on the person of the miracle worker but on the new world which is inaugurated by his ministry.

While this mode of interpretation is historically credible, it raises a hermeneutical question. What sense can we today make of the miracle stories if they signify the inbreaking of the reign of God, but miracles themselves are not occurring? Further, what difference would it make to a twentieth century person to know that in the first century a few blind people recovered their sight? What difference would it make to a woman whose son was drowned while trying to escape the political oppression of his country by taking a raft to sea, to know that Jesus once calmed a raging sea? Indeed, would it not make the permanently disabled feel cheated to know that someone with the same infirmity was healed in the first century, while his or her twentieth century life languishes?

While the ministry of healing was evidently part of the life of some branches of the early church,[7] the miracle stories were not broadcast only among those who might be medically benefitted. The miracle stories were preached among those who had no organic

4

defects but who could in some way be moved by the
stories.

5. Miracle Stories as Models of Ministry

Many contemporary church leaders, especially
those deeply committed to social reform, see the
miracle stories as models of ministry which illustrate
God's concern for the whole person and for the total
quality of that person's life. To heal blindness, for
example, was not only to restore sight but to destroy
the structure of power which kept that blind person
(and blind people) oppressed.

In preaching, we, as Jesus' followers, are ex-
horted to do battle with those forces which oppress
and dispossess individuals and groups. We are encouraged to bring about systemic change to upgrade the
total quality of life.

Change in social conditions is, indeed, an urgent
matter. However, such use of the miracle stories does
not always respect the integrity of the texts. For
the miracle stories themselves contain few admonitions
for the listener or reader to go and do as Jesus did.
At the level of oral tradition, the narrative style
of the stories invites the listener/reader to identify
with those who are <u>healed</u>. Other texts will admonish
our congregations to be healers, like the redactional
formulation of Mt. 10:7-8.

6. Miracle Stories as Models of Behavior

The behavior of a person healed in a miracle story
is sometimes held out as a model of behavior for a person in the modern congregation. The usual point of
contact is the element of risk.

The classic example is the story of Peter walking
on the water (Mt. 14:22-33/Mk. 6:45-52). What risks
can we take comparable to Peter stepping out of the
boat and onto the wind-whipped sea?

One cannot deny, of course, the element of risk
in a person breaking free of the established patterns
that accompany blindness or demon possession. Healing
upsets a familiar routine.

While risk taking is an essential element in personal growth and in attacking social evil, to use the text as a springboard for such exhortation is to lift up an element not found in the miracle stories themselves. Further, in this view the power of the story is dependent upon the hearer modifying his or her behavior. If the listener is not able to take the risk, the story becomes an impossible burden; the listener is weighted down by guilt. The miracle stories themselves do not impose a behaviorial burden but give the listeners or readers a reality out of which to live.

7. Miracle Stories as Stories

In light of recent insights from narrative theology, structuralism, literary criticism and the philosophy of language, the miracle stories may be interpreted as stories. We may interpret them in the same way that we interpret any story: listeners and readers enter into the world created by the narrative and join in its plot and movement. This approach requires that recipients be familiar with the rich background out of which the stories emerged.

To force all the miracle stories into one frame of reference is to take away from their individuality and uniqueness. One story may describe, in picture form, the meaning of a relationship with Jesus while another may function as a metaphor of healing.

This mode of interpretation is related to an older strata of scholarship which saw the miracle stories as embodying the self-understanding of the church. The older school, however, did not stress the narrative form of the story as constitutive to the meaning of the story.

In the following chapters, after suggesting a conceptual basis within which to understand the miracle stories, I seek to examine six miracle stories as stories. Hopefully, these studies will illustrate ways in which other miracle stories might be interpreted for preaching. In addition, I make suggestions for possible hermeneutical movements and offer sermons which illustrate how one preacher followed the path from exegesis to proclamation.

6

NOTES

[1] This chapter is not a "history of research" but recalls broad approaches which have percolated into the well of our appreciation of the miracle stories. On the difficulty of speaking of miracle, see Ian T. Ramsey, _Religious Language_ (New York: Macmillan, 1957), pp. 167-74. An expeditious, nontechnical overview is given in R.H. Fuller, _Interpreting the Miracles_ (London: SCM, 1963), pp. 8-18. For a review of theological assessments of the miracle stories see Ernst and Marie-Luise Keller, _Miracles in Dispute_, tr. M. Kohl (Philadelphia: Fortress, 1969). A brief but penetrating discussion is contained in Walter Wink, _Transforming Bible Study_ (Nashville: Abingdon, 1980), pp. 155-157.

[2] Indeed, in our own time, "advances" in our understanding of nature lead to continual reformulation of "the laws of nature."

[3] R.M. Grant, _Miracle and Natural Law in Graeco-Roman and Early Christian Thought_ (Amsterdam: North Holland, 1952).

[4] R.Bultmann and A. Wieser, "_pistis_," _Theological Dictionary of the New Testament_, ed. G. Kittel and G. Friedrich, tr. G. Bromiley (Grand Rapids: Eerdmans, 1968), vol. VI, pp. 182-96, 203-228; H.J. Hermisson and E. Lohse, _Faith_, tr. D. Stott (Nashville: Abingdon, 1981).

[5] Examples of such incidents are recorded in G. Delling, _Antike Wundertexte_ (Berlin: de Gruyter, 1960); P. Fiebig, _Antike Wundertexte_ (Bonn: Marcus and Weber, 1911); _idem_, _Juedische Wundergeschichten des neutestamentlichen Zeitalter_ (Tuebingen: Mohr, 1911).

[6] D.L. Tiede, _The Charismatic Figure as Miracle Worker_, SBL Dissertation Series (Missoula: Scholar's, 1972).

[7] E.g. Mt. 9:35; 10:1, 9-11, 14; Mk. 6:6-13; Lk. 9:1-6; I Cor. 12:9, 28: James 5:14.

CHAPTER II

STORY AS A LENS FOR INTERPRETING THE MIRACLE STORIES

"Story" is more than a literary classification.
With roots at the dawn of human consciousness, and
taking its pattern from life itself, story is an important form of human expression which speaks for us
and to us in two dimensions of human awareness: at the
level of conscious, rational, cognitive thought and at
the level of intuitive, imaginative, sense impression
and feeling.

This remarkable capacity of story derives from
the ways in which experience and expression are related. Story is not simply a shell which houses a
"point," a "lesson" or a "truth" in the way that a
shell houses a peanut. The full dimension of expression in a story is available to us only as we hear it
as a story.[1]

In this chapter I explore the nature of human
awareness, experience and knowledge as well as its expression in the form of story and I suggest implications for interpreting the miracle stories in
preaching. Without claiming that their insights are
exhaustive, I have been helped by the philosophy of
art of Susanne K. Langer and the larger understanding
of human culture set forth by Ernst Cassirer in which
Mrs. Langer's work found its own seedbed.

1. Three Modes of Human Awareness and Expression

Much human knowledge and awareness is symptomatic
of nothing more than the condition of the moment and[2]
much human expression simply signals that condition.
When our child's diapers are soaked, he is uncomfor-
table and he signals his discomfort with a penetrating
cry. On Sunday morning, when it is time to begin the
service of worship, the minister raises his or her
hands as a signal to the congregation to rise. There
is a one-to-one correspondence between the condition

9

and the signal. Without the presence of the stimu-
lating condition, no signal is given.

Beyond signalling is the ability to use symbols.
Of the difference between signal and symbol, Langer
writes,

> A sign is always embedded in reality, in a
> present that emerges from the actual past
> and stretches to the future; but a symbol
> may be divorced from reality altogether. It
> may refer to what is not the case, to a mere
> idea, a figment, a dream. It serves, there-
> fore, to liberate thought from the immediate
> stimuli of a physically present world; and
> that liberation marks the essential difference
> between human and nonhuman mentality.[3]

A symbol represents something else: a word, a figure,
a gesture, which represents another reality.

The mind can conceive of things, situations, persons, conditions, ideas which may not be immediately
present.[4] On a humid August day, when a piece of paper
sticks to my fingers like the back of a moistened pos-
tage stamp, I can sit in the office and imagine the
Christmas Eve service: candlelight, the smell of ever-
greens, a cello playing, "Lo How a Rose E'er Blooming."

Not only can I conceive of what that far-off
service might be like, but I can knock on the wall,
arouse my co-minister and spouse in the next office,
and tell her about it. The words we use are symbols
and when they are spoken they provoke the mind to conceive that which they represent.

Although language is governed by commonly accepted
rules of grammar and definition, the particular use of
a word is often made clear only by its context. In one
sermon the word "water" may refer to water flowing from
a gravel spring while in another sermon the same word
may refer to salt water from the ocean, to water stir-
ring as someone is immersed or to polluted water from
the Hudson River. By shuffling the same words, I can
create another meaning. To say, "God is love," is one
thing; to say, "Love is God," is quite another.

By watching a football official designate a penal-
ty with hand motions or by joining in a game of cha-
rades in which pantomime is used to denote a word, we
can see that such symbolic expression is not restricted

10

to spoken or written language. But within their particular contexts, such expressions still function on
the basis of one-to-one correspondence of symbol and
meaning.

At the same time, a great deal of human knowledge
and awareness is neither symptomatic of the moment nor
the result of the specific conceptual process
described above. This level of knowledge and awareness derives not from the pragmatic function of reason
and rationality but results from direct experience,
sense impression, intuition and the life of feeling.

I know, for instance, " . . . how a small fright
or 'startle' terminates, how the tensions of boredom
increase or give way to self entertainment, how day-
dreaming weaves in and out of realistic thought, how
the feeling of a place, a time of day, an ordinary
situation is built up."[5] I know what it is like to get
the doctor's report, to stand under a harvest moon in
the autumn leaves exchanging a first kiss, to feel as
though one door after another is closing on my life,
to contemplate the horror of nuclear war. I remember
the moment our first child heaved and kicked from the
womb. Such experiences inform and shape life and perception as surely as rational information gained from
the newspaper, from an instruction manual or from Sunday school.

An important breakthrough in our understanding of
such knowledge and expression is the discovery that
such intuitive experience and feeling is not merely an
irrational gush of emotion.

> . . . human feeling is a fabric, not a
> vague mass. It has an intricate, dynamic
> pattern, possible combinations, new
> emergent phenomena. It is a pattern of
> organically interdependent and interdeter-
> mined tensions and resolutions, a pattern
> of almost infinitely complex activation
> and cadence. To it belongs the whole
> gamut of our sensibility--the sense of
> straining thought, all mental attitude and
> motor set. Those are the deeper reaches
> that underlie the surface waves of our
> emotion and make human life a life of
> feeling instead of an unconscious metabolic
> existence interrupted by feelings.[6]

Thus, intuitive experience is a nonrational--but not an

11

irrational--source of knowledge.

In conventional conversation, the words we use to talk about intuitive knowledge are quite general. I may say, "It was such a joy!" But different experiences of joy have their own special character. Consider the difference in "joys" when a friend joins the church, when we hear the news of an imminent birth, when we hear the announcement of the resurrection at the funeral of an eighty-five year old who has fought the battle of life and won. Each has its own particular structure and force.

A symptom can be communicated by a signal. A concept can be communicated by a conventional symbol. Intuitive awareness can be expressed in forms appropriate to it.

Forms appropriate to intuitive awareness, especially myth and art, are presentational in nature. That is, in their appropriate media (e.g. dance, music, painting) they are presented to us without the need of interpretative statements. When they are presented, something is stirred in us though we may not be able to name the experience of being stirred in a satisfactory way.

Whereas a conventional symbol "stands in" for another reality, the reality expressed in a presentational form cannot be fully known except by means of the form itself. For, as Cassirer says, the presentational form "produces and posits a world of its own." Presentational forms are not "imitations but organs of reality."[7] Each form is "a particular way of seeing and carries within itself its particular and proper source of light."[8]

The most widely recognized presentational forms in the modern era are the arts.[9]

> Artistic symbols . . . are untranslatable; their sense is bound to the particular form which it has taken. It is always _implicit_ and cannot be explicated by any interpretation. This is true even of poetry, for though the _material_ of poetry is verbal, its import is not the literal association made in the words but _the way the assertion is made_, and this involves the sound, the tempo, the aura of associations of the words, the long or short sequences of ideas,

the wealth or poverty of transient
imagery that contains them, the sudden
arrest of fantasy by pure fact or of
the familiar fact by sudden fantasy,
the suspense of literal meaning by a
sustained ambiguity resolved in a
long-awaited key-word and the unifying,
all-embracing artifice of rhythm.[10]

Each mode of artistic expression is designed for a particular medium. A poem, for instance, is intended to
be heard or read. Ballet is designed for the eye and
a symphony for the ear.[11]

The creation of a presentational form begins when
a significant awareness "bursts forth" from the stream
of commonplace experience.[12] The creator then makes
an image of that feeling in another medium.

What any true artist . . . tries to
'recreate' is not a yellow chair, a hay
wain or a morally perplexed prince; as
'a symbol of his (sic) emotion,' but that
quality which he has once known, the
emotional 'value' that events, situations,
sounds or sights in their passing have had
for him. He need not represent those same
items of his experience, though psycho-
logically it is a natural thing to do if
they were outstanding forms; the rhythm
they let him see and feel may be projected
in other sensible forms, perhaps even
more purely.[13]

The presentational form allows the artist to create a
public representation of an otherwise private awareness.

When the artist creates an art form, only those
elements are used which are necessary to represent the
intuition. The artist includes everything that we need
to see, touch, hear, smell or feel in order to be
stirred by the work. A good piece is shaped economi-
cally but fully:

We grasp a work by giving ourselves to it. If it
is a symphony, we listen, and what we hear is the form
of the author's feeling. If it is a painting, we look
at it and what we see is a picture of the author's
feeling. If it is a poem, we imaginatively enter the

13

world created by the poem. We can talk about the poem
and if the poem is written in archaic or obtuse language, it may contain words that need to be explained,
but conversation about and explanation of the poem are
not substitutes for the experience of hearing the
poem.

We cannot always specify, in conventional language, the meaning of a piece. Indeed, Langer com-
plains that the study of presentational forms "has
been hampered and somewhat snarled by an unfortunate
'working model,' which is comment. The use of that
model has obscured the most distinctive characteristic
of art--that its import is not separable from the
form."[14]

The most appropriate means of grasping a piece is
to place ourselves so that the work can stir us in its
intended way. For the experience of "being stirred"
is the meaning of the work. Indeed, the work "cannot
be apprehended except by a corresponding dynamic process in ourselves."[15] The exact feeling which the
artist knows is not reproduced in us like a Xerox copy.
For each individual's life belongs uniquely to him or
to her. But a good piece kindles something in us akin
to that which was in the artist.

The process may be represented graphically:

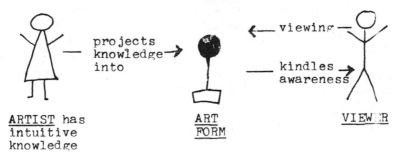

ARTIST has   ART   VIEWER
intuitive   FORM
knowledge

2. Story as Presentational Form

In the emergence of human culture, storytelling
precedes speech. The earliest forms of human expression are presentational; these include forms such as
dance, gesture, cave paintings, totemic objects and the
wails and whispers which precede song. Both Langer and
Cassirer conclude that these expressions are images of
intuitive awareness in much the same way as are works

14

of art.[16] Such images represent a feeling about a
special place, a particular event or life itself.

Further, the "first thing we do with images is to
envisage a story."[17] A dance around the campfire may
tell the story of a long past event which made a certain spot in the woods seem charged with a special
aura. The dance, of course, does not merely recount
the facts, but puts into the rhythmic movements of the
dancer, the feelings engendered by the association.
Since there was no speech to provide interpretative
commentary, the "meaning" of the dance was simply presented in the dance itself. Thus, Langer notes that
from the beginning of consciousness, "Pictures and
stories are the mind's stock in trade."[18]

The earliest evidence of speech is story expressed
in the form of myth.[19] Only a generation ago, myth was
regarded as a second-rate mode of expression and was
even described as a "disease of language." A mythic
tale was considered to be no more than a shabby overcoat which needed to be removed when the tale was
brought inside the house of the modern world view. According to the exacting criteria of the scientific
world view, myth contains naieve (and embarrassing)
conceptions of nature, science and history.

This understanding of myth has been superceded.
Myth promulgates neither science nor history in the
modern sense;[20] it is a form describing human feeling.
"The substratum of myth is not a substratum of thought
but of feeling."[21] In the form of story, a myth explains the various interrelationships of nature and
humankind, human beings with one another, and humankind with extra-human forces. Myth paints "word-
pictures" of the ways in which a person or a people
understand their experience. Often significant forces
are personified in the characters in the tale; sun
and moon may become metaphors conveying basic patterns
of life. Myth gives expression to what life in the
world feels like.

Without interpretative commentary, a myth is simply presented to its listeners or readers. "Word and
name do not designate and signify; they are and act."[22]
Myth is thus not an overcoat for an understanding of
reality but embodies that understanding. Those who
hear the myth find their own understanding of life
shaped by the myth. Myth thereby both reflects and
shapes consciousness. Persons begin to live and act
on the basis of the story.

15

This significant power to shape consciousness is retained as mental life develops and as the conventional, utilitarian use of language is separated from myth. But as the two forms of discourse become distinguishable, an additional dimension is added to the power of story. Because story is expressed in words, and words are the vehicles by which thought is conveyed, story can express both thought and intuition.

In the flow of the narrative, rational thought can be voiced in the minds and mouths of the characters as well as by the narrator. The context engages both the rational and the intuitive faculties because the story creates a "feeling context" in which to hear the words.[23] Story thus has the remarkable capacity to shape the whole of life, the Gestalt.

Story takes its form from life itself: event follows event, sometimes connected by cause and effect, in logical and predictible fashion, but sometimes in random fashion, with events following one another in completely unexpected ways. Story thus reflects the rhythm of life.

Stories are of different lengths and kinds, e.g. novel, short story, parable, joke, cartoon, movie, drama. Stories are not "given primarily to one particular sense, but to the imagination through whatever sense we employ to perceive and evaluate the action."[24] As we imaginatively enter the "world" created by the story, that which happens in the story happens to us. This immediate, experiential quality of story is the result of and the reason for many stories being told in the present tense--even stories which recall (or create) past events.[25]

When we hear a story, not only do we have an experience of the moment, but the story becomes a part of our reservoir of experience. It becomes a part of our personal (and often communal) history and memory.[26] Story thus has the power to enlarge our experience, history and memory. It allows us to try on other possible ways of living, thinking and feeling, much as I try on a new three-piece suit at the clothing store.

Although I may not have been present at certain events, and indeed, although such "events" may not have happened at all, hearing the story makes it as if they took place with me present. Although I did not live through the nuclear holocaust, through the stories of those who did, I can understand what it was like and it becomes a part of my memory.

The sources of stories are as rich as life itself. For example, the storyteller may begin with an actual personal experience, with an event which he or she witnessed, with one which was suggested to him or by another storyteller, by a dream or by an awareness which is best described in the mode of story. "The only condition is that materials from any source whatever must be completely put to artistic use, entirely transformed so that they do not lead away from the work but give it, instead, the air of being 'reality.'"[27]

When a story is based on an actual occurrence or fact, the story is not simply the record of that occurrence. The story creates an impression of what the precipitating occasion meant to the storyteller and what it can mean to the listeners of the story. A story is not as much report as interpretation, and it is not just cognitive interpretation but a form which embodies intuitive understanding. Thus, even if a miracle story is based on the actual occurrence of a miracle, the importance of the story is not its function as report but the way in which the story is told. The way the story is told reveals the significance of the event: the story makes that significance vicariously available to the listeners as their imaginations are engaged by the story.

The story-teller, while taking the model from life itself, organizes the narrative in such a way as to filter out distracting and unnecessary details. As I work the snow may be falling and the clock in the living room clicking, but these are incidental to what is happening in my imaginative life. Only those details are included in a story which will enhance the narrative image. Because of this, a story can often be more fully perceived than the jumble of happenings which comprise an ordinary person's life and history. That jumble does not always allow one to distinguish significant from insignificant, important from unimportant. A story, however, lifts up for our special attention a moment, an event, an awareness.

Of major importance, therefore, is the manner in which the story is told, especially the way its plot develops and the descriptive elements which are included and excluded.

Where the principle of narration enters
into poetic structure, all other devices

17

have to adjust themselves: the choice
of imagery is no longer free, as in the
pure lyric, but is determined by the
need of heightening some events and perhaps preparing for others, and of slowing
down or hurrying the course of action.
The descriptions of witchfires and water
snakes and 'slimy things' in the <u>Ancient
Mariner</u> make the story move with terri-
fying slowness while the ship is in the
doldrums.28

By giving attention to the essential discrete elements,
the storyteller can give fresh insight to even the
most familiar images and experiences.

It has often been said that the troubadours
(and their imitators) introduced their detailed accounts of weapons, and costumes,
tournaments, banquets and funerals for the
sheer pleasure of sensuous imagination.
But no matter how delightful these ingre-
dients are, they could no more be inserted
into a poem for their own sakes than an
extra pound of sugar could be happily
poured into a cake batter just because
sugar is so nice. They are, in fact,
powerful formal elements; they hold back
the narrative and cause the events to appear spread out as in a third dimension,
instead of racing to a conclusion 29

Descriptive elements not only slow and broaden the action, but they guide our feelings as we hear the
story. One metaphor may ring a firebell in the imagination while another may rub raw sensibility with a
cooling salve.

When interpreting a story, then, we need to give
careful attention to the detail with which it is told.
Details are chosen for their evocative power.

Thus, one can say, "the 'livingness' of a good
story is really much more, and often greater than, that
of actual experience."30 Stories, like all presentational forms, have the capacity to open unfelt reaches
of experience to us in such a way that hearing a story
may be as good as, if not better than, "being there."

3. Miracle Stories as Presentational Forms

The miracle stories of the synoptic gospels can be interpreted as presentational forms. For like other stories, the miracle stories project into narrative form human feeling from the life of the early church. They embody the feeling knowledge of the early church concerning various dimensions of the world in which the church lived.

In today's world, when we hear on the evening news about natural elements or diseases, their mention does little more than remind us of the physical condition of things. To a resident of the first century, however, miracle stories are more than weather reports or medical prognoses. In the first century, natural elements and diseases evoked responses deep in the life of feeling in a way in which such responses are not evoked today. In our scientifically oriented world, we have lost touch (on a day to day basis) with that feeling knowledge. However, careful interpretation can recover such vitality.

The process through which the miracle stories were shaped may be sketched thus:

BELIEVER
(or believing
community)
has awareness

— describes awareness →

MIRACLE
STORY

Hearing the miracle story today, with an ear attuned to that which the first century listener would have heard, evokes something of the same feeling in us:

MIRACLE
STORY

← hears story

feelings evoked →

LISTENER

The important question is how we in the twentieth century can develop the kind of sensitivity that will allow us to hear as the first century person would have heard.

In a work of art or in a myth, the creator provides all the details which are necessary for us to understand the work. Nothing more is needed. Ancient people apparently did not need to have the meaning of a myth explained to them. The meaning of the myth was communicated in the telling and in the hearing.

Likewise, recent research on the parables has indicated that the full and rich texture of the parables comes alive for us as we enter into their details and hear them as stories. Many parables, for instance, are comparisons. An unknown, such as the Reign of God, is compared with a known, such as the growth of a mustard seed. We do not shave a parable down to a point or a moral. In the first century, the parable communicated itself and its "meaning" came as "whole" with the story. The narrative form and meaningful content of the parable were unified like one's feeling and his or her experience.

In much the same way that we understand the parables, we can understand the import of miracle stories. Their meaning is communicated to us as we enter their rich detail. Notice: in the period of oral circulation, the gospel tradition does not provide interpretative statements about the miracle stories. Apparently in its preaching and teaching the church allowed the stories to interpret themselves. The detail and plot of the stories would cause the listeners to feel the scene and to have their own lives of feeling nurtured.

Our first task as preachers is to listen to the miracle stories with ears attuned to the first century in order to share the feelings evoked with our congregations. To do that, our exegesis can be guided by the question, "What feeling comes to expression in this story?" That question can be answered as we discover those feelings represented in the text and what echoes we can hear from the first century.

By being sensitive to the first century echoes, we can let analogous feelings to those of the early hearers be awakened in us. They are "analogous" because the cultural and historical situation has changed across the twenty centuries that separate us from the

miracle stories. For example, the same images which
may have caused a person to feel unclean in 30 A.D. may
not awaken a feeling of uncleanness in us. But perhaps something in our world will cause us to experience
much the same feeling. More importantly, we can take
note of how the early church found such a feeling resolved.

When we can describe the feelings from within
which the story emerged, then we can identify situations, contexts and images from our own culture which
arouse similar responses. In preaching, we want to
arouse feeling knowledge akin to that of the ancients.
And more, we want to let the "miracle" happen in the
life of feeling.

The miracle stories themselves suggest a way of
shaping the sermon. The miracle stories are simply
presented to the imagination, often in rich, sensual
detail. Through the enhancing and enlarging details,
the story comes alive without extraneous interpretative
remarks.

Rather than telling us in conventional language
what a miracle story means, the preacher could let the
sermon present itself to the imagination. For example,
rather than talking about uncleanness, the preacher
could use an image which captures the feeling of uncleanness. Let the plot of the miracle story itself
organize the flow of the sermon. The homiletical move,
then, would be from the feeling of uncleanness to the
experience of wholeness.

4. Exegesis of the Miracle Stories at the Level of
Oral Tradition

In regard to the first three gospels, Biblical interpreters commonly speak of a text having three
layers of development. It is sometimes possible to
identify the origin of a text in the life and ministry
of Jesus,[31] although this is notoriously difficult in
the case of the miracle stories. The second layer of
development is the preaching and teaching of the church
prior to the placement and use of a text in its present
literary and theological context. The final layer is
the creative editing, shaping and placement of the text
in its present place in the gospel where it serves the
purposes of the writers whom we know as Matthew, Mark
and Luke.

21

In preparing to preach from a text in the synoptic gospels, it is important for the preacher to make a deliberate decision about which layer of tradition will inform the sermon. Mark's use of a text may be quite different from the function of the text in the second layer of development. Both contain legitimate meanings, but each has its own integrity.

I focus on the miracle stories at the second layer of tradition. In order to determine the form of the story in that period, it is necessary to "peel away" words, phrases, themes and other evidences of editing and shaping which appear to have come from the hand of the gospel writer. A summary of this process with the resultant text is given in the first section of each of the succeeding chapters.

The studies of the individual miracle stories are controlled by the question, "What feeling comes to expression in this text?" I do not intend for this question to supplant other significant aspects of interpretation, but it does call attention to a dimension of the stories which has not been widely explored.

In focusing on the life of the miracle stories at the second layer of tradition, we cross into territory which has been staked out, in large measure, by form criticism. Based on the pioneering work of Rudolf Bultmann[32] and Martin Dibelius[33] a general consensus regarding the structure of the miracle stories prevailed for over fifty years. Until recently, form critics have not been as specific about the function of the stories as about their structure. Both yield important homiletical implications.

The consensus regarding the structure of the healing miracles and exorcisms may be outlined thus:

1. A description of the patient (and often of the setting).
2. A confrontation with the healer.
3. The healing itself (a touch, a word, etc.).
4. A demonstration that the healing has taken place.
5. A response to the healing such as an outburst of praise or gasp of wonder.

Some elements of the structure are missing from some

texts and other elements are added by other texts.

Other types of miracle stories manifest similar
typical features.[34] Influenced by structuralism, the
attempt to isolate the "deep structures" inherent in
language, recent critics have suggested more subtle
and complex structures for the miracle stories.[35]

While the form critics have not emphasized the
generative relationship between consciousness and its
expression in the form of the text, nevertheless, like
the structuralists, they have pointed to the close relationship between the structure of the text and its
function. A homiletical implication of both the classical discipline of form criticism and the atradition-
al approach of structuralism, is to keep the structure
of the sermon close to the structure of the text.

The structure of the text is not merely a topcoat
which can be left on the coatrack while the sermon
enters the sanctuary. The way in which the text unfolds is a part of the meaning of the text. Thus, in
preaching, when we honor the structure of the miracle
story by allowing the sermon to unfold in the same
scenes and plot as the text, we honor the meaning of
the text. And, further, the deep structures of the
miracle story are allowed to stir the deep structures
within us.

With respect to the function of the stories in the
community during the oral period, the early form-
critics saw the function of the miracle stories like
that of a calling card: the miracle stories called attention to the power of Jesus. And, the miracle stories were judged to have a missionary function as well.
"Preaching saved men (sic) and illustrated its points
by Paradigms. But the Tales (primarily miracle stories) . . . revealed self-convincing power. Both
types gained believers in Jesus 'the Lord.'"[36] The
miracle stories were thus not considered simply
"examples," but in their rich embroidery and detail,
the stories themselves could serve the function of
epiphany: they could manifest the power and presence of
the Lord.[37]

Critics of the last ten years have made a more delicate separation of the function of the stories. Gerd
Theissen in a sweeping, controversial and suggestive
work, sees the miracle stories in the oral tradition
reflecting the preoccupation of the lower social
classes with the limitations imposed on their

lifestyle.[38] The miracle stories describe the confidence that the enslaving powers of the old order, the hostile realities of the world, have been broken. The lower classes are then freed to claim a new life. The rebellion against the hostile world described in the miracle stories is rooted not in human longing but in that which was previously beyond the limits of experience.

While it is difficult to limit the origin of the miracle stories to lower classes, the attempt to relate the stories to particular settings has been well received. The precise settings, of course, will continue to be debated.

Professor Antoinette Wire, using structural and literary critical motifs, summarizes one of the most advanced statements on the settings of the stories.

> The narrative tells a marvelous break-
> through in the struggle against oppressive
> restrictions on human life. Exorcisms
> tell the overthrow of arbitrary, violent and
> total oppression, controversy miracles the
> expose' of violent moral and social re-
> striction, provision stories a break in the
> oppression of want and human resignation
> to it and demand stories the initiative
> that breaks out of physical and psycho-
> logical impotence. This struggle might
> be mapped in terms of a circle burst open
> or a mold broken.[39]

The miracle stories are thereby seen to witness to the experience of persons caught in closed systems which have now been opened by an extraordinary breakthrough. Others, still caught in such systems, can hear the miracle stories and feel the possibility of transformation.

Frequently in the studies that follow, I make reference to Ancient Near Eastern mythology, to Old Testament texts and to extra-Biblical literature. I do not claim direct literary dependence between these texts and the miracle stories. Rather, in the ancient milieu, the miracle stories would have evoked historical and mythological associations and feelings which may not be obvious to the modern interpreter.[40] I use such references to illuminate those ancient associations.

5. Matthew, Mark and Luke as Interpreters of the Miracle Stories.

While a full-scale redaction-critical analysis of the use of the miracle stories by the first three evangelists is outside the focus of this inquiry, it may be instructive to note the broad strokes with which the gospel writers interpret the miracle stories. In making such a sketch, we may draw upon scholarly consensus where it has emerged. I cite only representative literature with no attempt to be exhaustive.

The broadest base of consensus has gathered around the gospel of Matthew and is guided by the widely influential essay of H.J. Held.[41] Held finds patterns in Matthew's retelling of the miracle stories which provide indices to Matthew's purposes in using them. (1) Matthew abbreviates description of the characters and the setting and even omits some secondary characters. (2) Matthew expands the dialogue so that the dialogue is clearly the centerpoint of the stories.[43] Matthew often places the miracle stories in the gospel narrative so that they serve to illustrate larger themes which Matthew develops, particularly the themes of Christology, discipleship and faith.[44]

While the miraculous element is not altogether suppressed, Matthew clearly uses the stories for the instruction of the church. Indeed, Held concludes that the miracle stories function for Matthew as paradigms for the church. Those stories which illustrate the theme of Christology present the Christ of the miracle stories as the Lord who is still authoritative and active in the church.[45] Those stories which illustrate the theme of discipleship show that the disciples (i.e. the church) can and should do the same work as Jesus.[46] Those stories which illustrate the theme of faith show the listeners/readers both what Matthew believes true faith to be and the effect of that faith in the life of the one who practices it.[47]

Of course, in the individual tales these themes are developed with particular nuances and interpreters need to respect the particularity of the individual stories.[48] Further, John Heil cautions that miracle stories have a multidimensional character and that to reduce such stories to only one theme is to rob them of their richness and power.[49] For instance, Matthew may use the things which happen to characters in the stories as models of experience for the church. By

25

identifying with a character, like the leper of Mt. 8:
1-4, the church can "vicariously experience" the
"salvific presence" of Jesus.[50]

With respect to the miracle stories in the gospel
of Mark, the scholarly agreement is less impressive
but identifiable. Commentators point out that the
paradigm on which the gospel of Mark is based is the
apocalyptic scheme in which the world is under the
rule of Satan and his henchmen, the demons, whose purpose is to bind and restrict the life of the whole
cosmos. God has begun to break the back of Satan's
power and to plunder Satan's domain.[51]

Mark places the miracle stories in the service of
that major theme. Jesus challenges the power of Satan
in the world which now becomes a battleground between
the two. The exorcisms are instances, some say the
primary instances, of that battle.[52] And, indeed, a
careful examination of the vocabulary of Mark's miracle
stories reveals that nearly all are understood as
exorcisms. This is especially true of the nature
miracles and the healings.[53] In that battle, Jesus
emerges as "the stronger one."

Mark further places many of the miracle stories to
show that the power which was active in Jesus' miracle
working activity is also present in his teaching.[54]
This may be a polemical motif. Mark takes for granted
the presence of miracle workers in the culture (9:38-
40) and surely there were miracle workers in the
church. Miracle workers may reduce the apocalyptic
drama to the dramatic manifestations of the exorcisms.
Much of the content of Jesus' teaching in Mark emphasizes his suffering and the similar suffering of the
disciples. Mark may thus be balancing a theology
focused on the power of miracle working with one rooted
in the cross as the ultimate battleground between
Jesus and Satan. The disciples must fight on that
battleground, too.

A related concern is Mark's portrayal of the
disciples. Some authorities see Mark carrying out a
vendetta against the twelve.[55] Others see that the
twelve are presented only as lacking understanding.[56]
In the miracle stories in which the twelve appear in
a significant role, they are not model followers of
Jesus but desparately need instruction and correction. Indeed, in some cases their own infirmities of
faith need healing. Since miracle working was probably
a part of the life of Mark's church, it is likely that

Mark edits and places the stories in such a way as to help his or her church gain perspective on the miracle stories in light of the cross.[57]

Luke's use of the miracle traditions in the first volume has not been studied in detail.[58] Nevertheless, certain Lukan tendencies may be noted in the revision of the material. (1) Luke frequently places the word of Jesus and the miraculous deed on equal footing.[59] (2) Luke often omits details that would ordinarily draw attention to the characters other than Jesus and thus draws attention to Jesus himself.[60] (3) Luke sometimes highlights the recipients of the miracles when the recipients are not Jewish.[61] (4) The third evangelist accentuates the reaction of crowds as a response of praise to God for the mighty work.[62]

The two most important clues to Luke's use of the miracle stories are the programmatic statement of 4:16-30 and the placement of the stories in the narrative.[63] In his sermon at Nazareth, Jesus announces that the purpose of his ministry is to proclaim the good news of the Reign of God. The good news is that the Reign is beginning to dawn,[64] and Jesus illustrates its dawning by referring to two miracles of the Old Testament. Elijah fed the pagan widow of Zarephath and Elisha was responsible for the healing of the Gentile Namaan. The good news of the Reign is thus an announcement in both word and deed. The working of miracles is an important part of bringing the good news.

This is confirmed by the placement of the stories in the narrative. Immediately after the sermon at Nazareth, Jesus' first acts are healings which demonstrate his authority. He states his own mission, "I must preach the good news of the Reign of God . . . " (4:33). For Luke, preaching incorporates miracle working. When Jesus calls the first disciples, he does so with the miracle of the bursting nets (5:1-11). In 8:1 his work is described as "preaching and bringing the good news of the Reign of God;" immediately he teaches (8:4-21) and then works miracles (8:22-56). Having thus demonstrated what it means to bring the good news, he invests the twelve with authority (4:32) and charges them to go forth preaching the Reign and healing (9:1-2).[65] Much the same charge is given to the seventy who are sent. The connection between healing and the Reign is made even more clear. "Heal the sick (in the town) and say to them, 'The Reign of God has come near to you.'" (10:10). It may not be too much to claim that for Luke a miracle is a

mini-instance of the coming of the Reign. The coming
of the Reign in its fullness will be like the experience of healing, exorcism or calming.

The importance of this presentation becomes clear
in the book of Acts. For in the second volume, Luke
seems to regard the ministry of Jesus as a paradigm
for the ministry of the church.[67] The authority
invested in Jesus and the twelve and the seventy is now
invested in the church.

NOTES

[1]Recent Biblical study has been marked by similar
interest in the unity of form and meaning in the text.
This is especially true of investigation of the metaphorical nature of the parables and sayings of Jesus,
e.g. R.W. Funk, Jesus as Precursor (Philadelphia: Fortress, 1975); R. Tannehill, The Sword of His Mouth
(Philadelphia: Fortress, 1975); J.D. Crossan, In
Parables (New York: Harper and Row, 1973); B.B. Scott,
Jesus, Symbol-Maker for the Kingdom (Philadelphia:
Fortress, 1981). The structuralists are opening windows on our understanding of the relationship between
the structures of narratives and the deep structures
of existence which give rise to texts, e.g. D. Patte,
What Is Structural Exegesis (Philadelphia: Fortress,
1976); D. and A. Patte, Structural Exegesis from Theory
to Practice (Philadelphia: Fortress, 1978); J. Calloud,
Structural Analysis of Narrative (Philadelphia: Fortress, 1976). Literary criticism calls attention to the
interpretation of texts as literature, e.g. W.A.
Beardslee, Literary Criticism of the New Testament
(Philadelphia: Fortress, 1970); N.R. Peterson, Literary
Criticism for New Testament Critics.(Philadlephia:
Fortress, 1978); D. Via, The Parables (Philadelphia:
Fortress, 1967). I am indebted to such emphases more
than the footnotes will show. However, as interpretative methods, these often seem to focus on the text qua
text without significant reference to traditional historical questions. While this focus sharpens our perception of some aspects of the text, it may also e-
liminate from consideration other eye-opening elements
of interpretation. For more detailed critique, see
C. Carlston, "Parable and Allegory Revisited," CBQ 43
(1981), pp. 228-242.

[2]E. Cassirer, *An Essay on Man* (New Haven: Yale, 1944), pp. 31-41; *idem.*, *The Philosophy of Symbolic Forms*, tr. R. Manheim (New Haven: Yale, 1955) vol. III, pp. 2ff. S.K. Langer, *Philosophy in a New Key* (Cambridge: Harvard, 1957), pp. 29ff.; Charles Morris, *Signs, Language and Behaviour* (New York: Prentice-Hall, 1946), pp. 23ff.

[3]S.K. Langer, "The Lord of Creation," *Fortune* 20, no. 1 (1944), p. 140. Cf. *Philosophy in a New Key*, p. 61.

[4]Cassirer, *An Essay on Man*, pp. 31-41; *The Philosophy of Symbolic Forms*, vol. I, pp. 177ff., Langer, *Philosophy in a New Key*, pp. 79-102.

[5]S.K. Langer, *Mind* (Baltimore: Johns Hopkins, 1967), vol. I, p. 57; cf. pp. 55-69. S.K. Langer, *Problems of Art* (New York: Scribner's, 1950), p. 22.

[6]S.K. Langer, *Philosophical Sketches* (Baltimore: Johns Hopkins, 1962), p. 89. "In the first place, the phenomenon usually described as a 'feeling' is really that an organism feels something . . . is a process, perhaps a large complex of processes within the organism. Some vital activities of great complexity and high intensity usually (perhaps always) involving nervous tissue, are felt," *Mind*, vol. I, p. 21.

[7]E. Cassirer, *Language and Myth*, tr. S.K. Langer (New York: Dover, 1955), p. 8.

[8]*Ibid.*, p. 11.

[9]In the development of human consciousness, the earliest presentational forms are dance, gesture, song and plastic representation such as the cave paintings and the creation of totemic objects. Cassirer, *The Philosophy of Symbolic Forms*, vol. II, p. 38. Cf. his *Language and Myth*.

[10]*Philosophy in a New Key*, p. 260. Cf. Cassirer, *An Essay on Man*, pp. 136-70.

[11]On the appropriate media of the arts, see S.K. Langer, *Feeling and Form* (New York: Scribner's, 1953). The arts " . . . exist only for the sense or the imagination that perceives them" (p. 50).

[12]*Language and Myth*, p. 38. Theologically, we might describe such moments as "revelation." For in

them we perceive life and its meaning in dynamic new ways.

[13]Mind, vol. I, p. 118.

[14]Feeling and Form, p. 394. "The direct perception of artistic import . . . is not systematic . . . It is intuitive, immediate and its deliverances are ineffable." Cf. Mind, vol. I, p. 65.

[15]An Essay on Man, p. 151.

[16]Cassirer, The Philosophy of Symbolic Forms, vol. II, pp. 38ff. "It has been rightly stressed that rite precedes myth" (p. 38). For a detailed reconstruction of the emergence of expression, see Langer, Mind (Baltimore: Johns Hopkins, 1972), vol. II, pp. 265-355. Cf. Mind, vol. I, pp. 131-137. "Undoubtedly the first outward show of sacred emotions is purely self-expressive, an unconscious issue of feelings into shouting and prancing and rolling on the earth like a baby's tantrum; but soon the outward burst becomes a habitual reaction and is used to demonstrate, rather than to relieve, the feelings of individuals. Lively demonstration makes an emotion contagious. Shout answers shout. The collective prancing becomes dancing. Even those who are not compelled by the inner tension to let off steam just at this moment, fall into step and join the common cry. But as soon as an expressive act is performed without inner momentary compulsion, it is no longer self-expressive: it is expressive in a logical sense. It is not a sign (signal) of the emotion it conveys, but a symbol of it. Instead of completing the natural history of a feeling, it denotes the feeling and may merely bring it to mind, even for the actor" (Philosophy in a New Key, p. 129).

[17]Langer, Philosophy in a New Key, p. 145.

[18]Ibid., p. 146.

[19]Cassirer, The Philosophy of Symbolic Forms, vol. II, passim., Language and Myth, pp. 23-63; Langer, Philosophy in a New Key, pp. 171-203.

[20]Cassirer, The Philosophy of Symbolic Forms, vol. III, pp. 58-91. In order to understand a particular expression, we start with "the formations in which it exists and consists" (p. 57).

[21]Cassirer, An Essay on Man, p. 81.

[22]Cassirer, _The Philosophy of Symbolic Forms_, vol. II, p. 40.

[23]"The occurrence of thought is an event in a thinker's personal history, and has as distinctive a qualitative character as an adventure, a sight or a human contact; it is not a proposition, but the entertainment of one, which necessarily involves vital tensions, feelings, the imminence of other thoughts and the echoes of past thinking" (Langer, _Feeling and Form_, p. 219).

[24]_Ibid._, P. 355.

[25]_Ibid._, p. 303.

[26]_Ibid._, p. 263.

[27]_Ibid._, p. 245.

[28]S.K. Langer, "The Primary Illusions and the Great Orders of Art," _Hudson Review_ 3 (1950), p. 231.

[29]_Feeling and Form_, p. 283-84.

[30]_Ibid._, p. 285.

[31]Much of the material credited to the life and ministry of Jesus is from the sayings traditions. For a summary of criteria used to assign statements to the historical Jesus, see N. Perrin, _Rediscovering the Teaching of Jesus_ (New York: Harper and Row, 1967), pp. 15-49.

[32]_The History of the Synoptic Tradition_, tr. J. Marsh (Oxford: Blackwell, 1962), pp. 209-244.

[33]_From Tradition to Gospel_, tr. B.L. Woolf (New York: Scribner's, 1934), pp. 70-103.

[34]The classification of the miracle stories is in transition. Bultmann proposed four categories: exorcism, healing, raising from the dead and nature miracle (pp. 231-235). More recent critics suggest more fluid and complex classifications.

[35]E.g. R.W. Funk, "The Form of the New Testament Healing Miracle," _Semeia_ 12 (1978), pp. 57-96; A.C. Wire, "The Structure of the Gospel Miracle Stories and Their Tellers," _Semeia_ 11 (1978), pp. 83-114; the

first part of Gerd Theissen, <u>Urchristliche Wunder-geschichten</u> (Guetersloh: Gerd Mohn, 1974) and H.D. Betz, "The Early Christian Miracle Story: Some Observations on the Form Critical Problem," <u>Semeia</u> 11 (1978) pp. 69-82.

[36]Dibelius, p. 96, my emphasis. Dibelius concludes that the embroidery of the Tales shows that they were told for the sheer joy of telling. He traces the origin of the miracle Tales to the Paradigms (example stories used in preaching). A miracle story, to him, is a Paradigm expanded.

[37]<u>Ibid</u>., p. 103.

[38]While Theissen's <u>Urchristliche Wundergeschichten</u> remains untranslated, its main ideas are available in reviews by Hendrikus Boers and Paul Achtemeier, <u>Semeia</u> 11 (1978), pp. 1-68. Theissen discusses these theses in detail under the rubrics of social function, religious function and existential function.

[39]Wire, p. 109. While Professor Wire's study is very suggestive, she does not posit concrete situations in the first century for which the four types of stories would be appropriate.

[40]Analogously, N. Perrin traces the mythical roots of the symbol Reign of God in his <u>Jesus and the Language of the Kingdom</u> (Philadelphia: Fortress, 1976), pp. 16ff.

[41]"Matthew as Interpreter of the Miracle Stories," G. Bornkamm, G. Barth and H. Held, <u>Tradition and Interpretation in Matthew</u>, tr. P. Scott (Philadelphia: Westminster, 1963), pp. 165-300. The genesis of Held's proposal is found in J. Schniewind, <u>Das Evangelium nach Matthaeus</u> (Goettingen: Vandenhoeck and Ruprecht, 1936), pp. 36, 106.

[42]<u>Held</u>, pp. 168-181, 233.

[43]<u>Ibid</u>., pp. 193-206, 233-237.

[44]<u>Ibid</u>., pp. 168-206, 237-238.

[45]<u>Ibid</u>., pp. 246-52, 270-274.

[46]<u>Ibid</u>., p. 250, 270-74.

[47] Ibid., pp. 239, 275-95.

[48] While the details of Held's analysis are frequently subjected to scrutiny and refinement, his major conjecture that Matthew uses most of the miracle stories as paradigms has been largely accepted. J.D. Kingsbury, "Observations on the Miracle Chapters of Matthew 8-9," CBQ 40 (1978), pp. 559-60, reports that the three major attempts to interpret the miracle stories all derive from Held. Further literature is cited in the critical study of J.P. Heil, "Significant Aspects of the Healing Miracles in Matthew," CBQ 41 (1979), pp. 274-87. Cf. the commentaries ad. loc.

[49] Heil, pp. 280-81. Heil rightly emphasizes that all elements of a miracle story must be kept in full view in order to achieve satisfactory interpretation.

[50] Ibid., pp. 282-283.

[51] A recent representative statment is Neill Q. Hamilton, Recovery of the Protestant Adventure (New York: Seabury, 1981), pp. 71-106. Cf. James M. Robinson, The Problem of History in Mark, SBT First Series 13 (London: SCM, 1957), pp. 33-42, and K.M. Fisher and U.C. von Wahlde, "The Miracles of Mark 4:35-5:43," Biblical Theology Bulletin, 11 (1981), p. 13. For overview of recent approaches to Mark, see J.D. Kingsbury, "The 'Divine Man' as the Key to Mark's Christology-- The End of an Era?" Interpretation 35 (1981), pp. 243-257. For a method of investigating the miracle stories in Mark, see Paul J. Achtemeier, Mark. Proclamation Commentaries (Philadelphia: Fortress, 1975), pp. 75-77.

[52] Robinson, pp. 33-34; Hamilton, pp. 80-85.

[53] Fisher and van Wahlde; pp. 14-15, Hamilton, p. 81; R.E. Brown, "The Gospel Miracles," in The Bible in Current Catholic Thought, ed. J.L. Mackenzie (New York: Herder and Herder, 1962), pp. 187ff.

[54] Achtemeier, p. 81.

[55] T.J. Weeden, Mark: Traditions in Conflict (Philadelphia: Fortress, 1971), pp. 23-51, who sees the twelve as representing not the historical twelve but heretical leaders of the church to whom Mark was writing.

[56] Most of the commentaries, ad loc.

[57]On the disciples in Mark, see Achtemeier, pp. 101-110 and Hamilton, pp. 106-210.

[58]The major contribution is Paul J. Achtemeier, "The Lukan Perspective on the Miracles of Jesus: A Preliminary Sketch," Perspectives on Luke-Acts, ed. C. Talbert (Edinburgh: T & T Clark, 1978), pp. 153-167.

[59]Ibid., p. 155.

[60]Ibid.

[61]Ibid., p. 156.

[62]Ibid.

[63]Ibid., p. 156, calls attention to these details but the value judgment is mine.

[64]"Today this Scripture has been fulfilled in your hearing." Cf. H. Conzelmann, The Theology of St. Luke, tr. G. Buswell (New York: Harper and Rown, 1961), p. 36.

[65]By investing the twelve with authority, Jesus enables them to do that which he is able to do. J.A. Fitzmyer, The Gospel According to Luke I-IX, AB (Garden City: Doubleday, 1981), pp. 542-43; I.H. Marshall, Commentary on Luke, NIGTC (Grand Rapids: Eerdmans, 1978), p. 178.

[66]The theme of authority reappears in 10:19, but note, 10:20, that the seventy are not to be overly impressed with the authority in itself.

[67]E.g. Acts 2:22, 43; 5:12; 6:8; 14:3; 15:12.

CHAPTER III

THE STILLING OF THE STORM

Mark 4:35-41

1. Recovering the Oral Tradition

Major interpreters agree that vss. 35-36a are a seam fashioned by Mark to knit the story into its present context.[1] Vs. 36b has been shaped by Mark to make the whole scene coincide with 4:1 in which we find Jesus in a boat.[2] The phrase "as he was" interrupts the flow of the story and is likely a Markan parenthetical clause.[3] The question of vs. 41, likewise, is a Markan theme and does not belong to the original strata,[4] as is perhaps the case with the question of vs. 40.

The text would read roughly as follows.

(36b) They took Jesus with them in a boat. (37) And a great storm of wind arose and the waves beat into the boat so that the boat was filling. (38) But he was asleep in the stern on a cushion; and they woke him and said to him, "Teacher, do you not care if we perish?" (39) And he awoke and rebuked the wind and said to the sea, "Peace! Be still!" And the winds ceased and there was a great calm. (41) And they were filled with awe.

2. Interpretation of the Story

The searchlights of commentators have focused on an aspect of this pericope which is significant for our interpretation: the background in the history of religions. This clue helps us identify the feeling which the story embodies.

Scholars customarily point to passages from the Psalms which stress the terror of the sea and the wind and God's mastery of these phenomena as the background for interpretation.[5] Paul Achtemeier points out, furthur, that the social and mythological associations with the sea and with storms on the sea have roots deep in Near Easter mythology, especially in the epic Enuma Elish.[6]

In that ancient myth, which is told to account for the creation of the world and the origin of the Babylonian gods, we notice that at the beginning of the drama, the action takes place in the universe; the gods of the story are not only characters but, as D.W. Thomas says, " . . . they are personifications of it (i.e. the universe)."[7] Indeed, Apsu and Tiamat, two of the leading characters of the drama "speak and move about . . . fight or are fought, even as we may read of it in the epic, are otherwise two great Seas who existed in the beginning when all was water."[8] A third character is Mummu who, when not serving as counsellor to Apsu, is cloud, mist or fog. The water, then, is the unformed primeval chaos.

As the drama unfolds, Tiamat and a coterie of rebel gods and their subalterns prepare for war against the established gods. Two great warrior gods, Ea and Anu, are sent against Tiamat.[9] But their strength is insufficient to stand up to the rebel goddess. The power of the rebel sea is thus underscored when neither earth nor sky is able to overcome her.

The situation looks hopeless when the hero Marduk comes into the fray. He prepares himself for the battle: among his weapons are the winds and the flood-storm. It is a desperate battle which comes to a climax in a bloody scene in which Marduk confronts Tiamat face-to-face. Her senses leave her and in a few swift movements she is dead. Marduk carves order out of the chaos of her body: half the sea-dragon becomes the sky which keeps back the primordial waters while the other half is made into land with primordial waters beneath it. Guards are posted in order to bar the waters of chaos from trespassing their newly created boundaries.

In a related mythological epic, Gilgamesh, we read of one who must navigate flood waters to find eternal life.[11] Mythology, then, seems to give expression to primitive fear of the sea. Water represents primeval chaos.

While the Hebrew people did not share the view
that creation was acheived by the violent overcoming
of chaos, scholars have argued that the image of the
primeval sea lies behind Genesis 1:1.[12] The sea was
in a perpetual state of storm.

Strands of the Old Testament reflect memories of
the sea as a place of chaos and conflict. The Lord
battles Rahab in the sea (Job 26:12; Ps. 89:10). God
is the one who shall slay the dragon of the sea (Is.
27:1). The sea is like one of the enemies of God
(Ps. 72:8). God divided the sea with his strength
(Ps. 74:13). God shut the sea within doors (Job 38:8)
and assigned the sea its limits (Ps. 8:29; Jer. 5:22).
The sea is personified and speaks (Is. 28:14). Frequently the Lord is described as ruling over the
raging of the sea[13] and the raging of the wind.[14] Ps.
107:23-30 particularly pictures Jewish feeling about
the sea.

Many of these fearful associations were very much
alive in the religious literature of the period in
which the story of the stilling of the storm was
formed. The Qumran community sang:

> (I am) as a sailor in a ship
>   amid furious seas;
> their waves and all their billows
>   roar against me.
> (There is) no calm in the whirlwind
>   that I may restore my soul,
> no path that I may straighten my way
>   on the face of the waters.
> The deeps resound to my groaning
>   and (my soul has journeyed) to the
>   gates of death. (IQH VI)[15]

The hymn uses the sea in a comparison: the singer is
like one who finds terror on the sea.

In IV Ezra, a dream reports that the sea is the
source of an eagle which is responsible for reprehen-
sible acts on the earth. The eagle brings all manner
of chaos.

In the messianic apocalypse of II Baruch, the
waters are vividly described.

> And when I had said these things I fell
> asleep, and I saw a great vision and
> lo! a cloud was ascending from a very

great sea, and I kept gazing upon it,
and lo!, it was full of waters white
and black . . . and I saw the cloud passing
swiftly in quick courses and it covered
all the earth. And it came to pass after
these things that the cloud began to pour
upon the earth waters that were in it.
And I saw that there was not one and the
same likeness in the waters that were in
it. And I saw that the waters became
bright, but they were not many, and after
these things again I saw black waters . . .
and it came to pass at the end of the cloud
that lo! it rained black waters and they
were darker than had been all those waters
that were before, and fire was mingled
with them and when those waters descended,
they wrought devastation and destruction
. . . (53:1-12, passim).[16]

In the interpretation of the vision, the waters sym-
bolize the world's history from Adam to messiah (56:1).
The black waters are the rebellion of Adam (58:8-16),
the weighing of sin (58:1), etc. The language symbol-
lically expresses the author's meaning.

The Testament of Naphtali pictures a visionary
experience centered around a boat in a storm.

And again, after seven days, I saw our
father Jacob, standing by the sea of
Jamnia, and we were with him. And behold, there came a ship sailing by without
sailors or pilot; and there was written
upon the ship, The Ship of Jacob. And
our father said to us, Come let us em-
bark on our ship. And when he had gone
on board, there arose a vehement storm,
and a mighty tempest of wind; and our
father, who was holding the ship, departed
from us. And we, being tossed with the
tempest, were borne along the sea; and
the ship was filled with water and was
pounded by the mighty waves, until it
was broken up. And Joseph fled away upon
a little boat, and we were all scattered
unto the ends of the earth. Then Levi,
girt about with sackcloth, prayed for
us all unto the Lord. And when the storm
ceased, the ship reached land as it were
in peace. And lo, our father came and

we all rejoiced with one another. (6:1-8).[17]

In Daniel 7:2, four great beasts arise from the sea. Revelation 13:1 pictures a beast rising out of the sea and at 21:1 the sea is said to be no more. Jude 13 describes people as wild waves of the sea who are casting up the foam of their own sin.[18]

Those who would hear the story of the stilling of the storm would bring with them this rich background. In this sense, the story is charged with human feeling.

In the gospel story, the response of the disciples to the storm is just what we would expect: they are terrified. Jesus responds, as all commentators note, with a word which is usually applied to demons: "Be still!"[19] The power which is raging against the boat is thus implicitly acknowledged to be more than a weather front.[20]

As the pericope climaxes, attention is drawn to the religious state of the onlookers. They are filled with awe. Long ago, Rudolf Otto made clear that awe is a response of the inner life as well as of the mind. "The awe . . . may indeed be so overwhelmingly great that it seems to penetrate to the very marrow, making the man's (sic) hair bristle and his limbs quake."[21] This is very much the sense of the phrase in the New Testament period.[22]

The story directs a new word to the fear of the power of chaos: be still. In Christ, the fear of being overcome by chaos has been released.

In a short but definitive article, Gunther Bornkamm points out that Matthew links the sayings on discipleship (8:18-22) with the stilling of the storm by means of the lynch-pin "follow." By placement and revision of the tale itself (8:23-27), Matthew uses the story to illustrate the situation of the church: like the disciples in the storm-tossed boat, the church is in a life-threatening situation. But, the church should take courage because Jesus is present. The story is thus an example for the congregation.[23]

Mark uses the technical expressions for exorcism, "rebuke" and "be still," to make clear that the storm at sea is a battleground between the elemental forces of Satan and the one through whom God's reign is beginning to dawn.[24] Even though the disciples have just had a private audience in which Jesus explained "everything" to them (4:34), they still do not understand the real nature of their situation with Jesus. They are afraid, even in his presence.

Luke (8:22-25) shaves away extraneous material so as to focus all eyes and ears on Jesus. He is the master.[25] In contrast to Mark who presents the disciples as lacking faith, Luke pictures them as having forgotten their faith in the crush of the moment. Luke may be using the story (and those that follow) so that when the twelve are sent forth (9:1), they will understand the nature and extent of their authority, which comes from the one who calmed the storm.

3. The Use of the Story in Preaching

What, in the world of my congregation, functions like the sea in the world of the first century church? What situation or news causes me to feel like I am helpless, on a boat which is beginning to sink into the belly of the sea? Sometimes we do feel overwhelmed by forces in the world which are stronger than we.

In the gospel story, the cause of such fear is concrete: the chaotic power of the sea. In our preaching we need to be equally concrete and to specify situations which provoke us to the feeling of being overwhelmed.

The characters with whom we identify in the story are the disciples. They (and we) need to feel the storm calmed.

Besides identifying situations which arouse the feeling of being on a sinking ship, we want to identify how a relationship with Jesus and the church can relieve such feelings. In the language of the story, how can we feel the wind and the waves subside?

NOTES

[1] A summary of evidence and bibliography is given in E.J. Pryke, Redactional Style in the Marcan Gospel (Cambridge: The University Press, 1978), pp. 13, 157; Rebecca Patten, The Thaumaturgical Element in the Gospel of Mark, unpublished Ph.D. Dissertation, Drew

University, 1976, pp. 79-81; Priscilla Patten, <u>Parable</u> <u>and Secret in the Gospel of Mark in the Light of</u> <u>Select Apocalyptic Literature</u>, unpublished Ph.D. Dissertation, Drew University, 1976. For development of methodology, R.H. Stein, "The Proper Methodology for Ascertaining a Marcan Redactionsgeschichte," NT 13 (1971), pp. 161-198.

[2]Pryke, pp. 13, 157; R. Patten, p. 80.

[3]Pryke, pp. 32ff.

[4]<u>Ibid</u>., pp. 13, 157.

[5]Some scholars attempt to equate Jesus' power with God's power while others contend that the incident shows that the same power at work in creation is also at work in the ministry of Jesus. See Fuller, p. 53; A. Richardson, <u>The Miracle Stories of the Gospels</u> (London: SCM, 1941), p. 93; H. van der Loos, <u>The</u> <u>Miracles of Jesus</u> (Leiden: Brill, 1965), p. 648; F. Hauck, <u>Das Evangelium des Markus</u> (Leipzig: Diechertsche 1931), p. 61; E. Klostermann, <u>Das Markasevangelium</u> (Tuebingen: Mohr, 1950), p. 45; J. Schniewind, <u>Das</u> <u>Evangelium nach Markus</u> (Goettingen: Vandenhoeck and Ruprecht, 1936); W. Grundmann, <u>Das Evangelium nach</u> <u>Markus</u> (Berlin: Evangelische, 1959), p. 103: E. Schweizer, <u>The Good News According to Mark</u>, tr. D.H. Madvig (Richmond: John Knox, 1970), p. 109. E. Lohmeyer, <u>Das Evangelium des Markus</u> (Goettingen: Vandenhoeck and Ruprecht, 1951), p. 89, but V. Taylor, <u>The</u> <u>Gospel According to St. Mark</u> (London: Macmillan, 1952), p. 272.

[6]P. Achtemeier, "Person and Deed: Jesus and the Storm Tossed Sea," Interp 16 (1962), pp. 169-76. Lohmeyer, p. 89, and Klostermann, p. 46, notice that the pericope contains a number of Semetisms which suggests a Palestinian influence.

[7]D. Thomas, <u>Documents from Old Testament Times</u> (London: Nelson, 1958), p. 4. The full text is given in J. Pritchard, <u>The Ancient Near East</u>: An Anthology of Texts and Pictures (Princeton: Princeton University Press, 1958), vol. I.

[8]Thomas, p. 4.

[9]Ea personifies the earth and Anu the sky. The primeval superiority of the sea is evident.

[10]Similar myths in related cultures are discussed by O, Kaiser, *Die mythische Bedeutung des Meer* (Berlin: Toepelmann, 1962) and A. Wensinck, *The Ocean in the Literature of the Western Semites* (Wiesbaden: Sandig, 1968). Cf. M. Wakeman, "Chaos," IDB Supplementary Volume, pp. 143-145.

[11]Pritchard, pp. 40-75.

[12]H. Gunkel, *Genesis* (Goettingen: Vandenhoeck and Ruprecht, 1922), p. 102; C. Westermann, *Genesis 1-11* (Neukirchener-Vluyn: Neukirchener, 1974), pp. 104ff.; G. von Rad, *Genesis*, rev. ed., tr. J. Marks (Philadelphia: Westminster, 1971), pp. 49-50.

[13]e.g. Ps. 29:3; 33:7; 46:3; 65:7; 77:17.

[14]e.g. Ps. 147:18; Prov. 30:4; Job 28:25; Am. 4:13; Is. 27:8.

[15]Quoted from G. Vermes, *The Dead Sea Scrolls in English* (Baltimore: Pelican, 1962).

[16]References to pseudepigraphic writings are from R. Charles, *The Apocrypha and Pseudepigrapha of the Old Testament* (Oxford: Clarendon, 1913), vol. II.

[17]Other Jewish storm traditions are no earlier than the second century. See Fiebig, *Juedische Wundergeschichten*, p. 61.

[18]II Baruch 29:4 and IV Ezra 6:51 describe the killing of the sea-dragon which is given to the redeemed to eat. Ecclesiasticus 43:23 recounts that God stilled the deep. T. Ash. 7:3 says that the Messiah will break the head of the dragon who lives in the water.

[19]E. Stauffer, "*epitimao*," TDNT, vol. II, p. 624, cites texts from Judaism which depict God rebuking the elements as well as the demonic. Lohmeyer, p. 89; Grundmann, p. 105; Klostermann, p. 46; Hauck, p. 62; Schweizer, p. 109; Taylor, p. 276.

[20]D. Nineham, *Saint Mark* (London: Penguin, 1963), p. 147; Grundmann, p. 105; Klostermann, p. 46; Hauck, p. 62; Taylor, p. 276; Schweizer, p. 109; G. Schille, "Die Seesbeermerzahlung," ZNW 56 (1965), p. 36, though contrast P. Harle, "Le tempete apaises; notes exegetiques sur cette pericope synoptique a trois tremoins,"

Foi et Vie 65 (1966), p. 84.

[21]The Idea of the Holy, tr. J. Harvey (London: Oxford, 1950), p. 16.

[22]J. Balz, "phobeo," TDNT, Vol. IX, pp. 205-208. Further, G. van der Leeuw, Religion in Essence and Manifestation. tr. J. Turner (New York: Harper Torchbooks, 1963), p. 48, who writes, "The expression adopted must be a very general one since it is question of establishing an attitude which includes the whole personality at all its levels and in countless nuances." Cf. p. 28.

[23]"The Stilling of the Storm in Matthew," in Bornkamm, Barth and Held, Tradition and Interpretation in Matthew, pp. 52-57, followed by Held, pp. 200ff., 210, 233, 246, 249f., 265, 267, 284 and most other commentators. F.W. Beare, The Gospel According to Matthew (San Francisco: Harper and Row, 1981), p. 216; E. Schweizer, The Good News According to Matthew, tr. D. Green (Atlanta: John Knox, 1975), p. 222; H.C. Waetjen, The Origin and Destiny of Humanness (Corte Madera: Omega, 1976), pp. 119-121; P. Ellis, Matthew: His Mind and His Message (Collegeville: Liturgical, 1974), p. 43; K. Stendahl, "Matthew," Peake's Commentary on the Bible, ed. M. Black and H. Rowley (London: Nelson, 1962), p. 781; J.C. Fenton, Saint Matthew (London: Penguin, 1963), p. 130; but contra R. Gundry, Matthew: A Commentary on His Literary and Theological Art (Grand Rapids: Eerdmans, 1981), p. 154.

[24]Robinson, p. 40; Nineham, p. 148; Achtemeier, Mark, p. 81; Hamilton, p. 84; Fisher and von Wahlde, p. 13; H.C. Kee, "The Terminology of Mark's Exorcism Stories," NTS 14 (1968), pp. 232-46.

[25]Whether the storm is to be understood as the work of demons is debated. Contrast Conzelmann, Theology of Saint Luke, p. 149, with the better arguments of Fitzmyer, p. 730; Marshall, p. 334; Achtemeier, "Perspectives," p. 163; E.E. Ellis, The Gospel of Luke (Greenwood, S.C.: Attic, 1966), p. 130.

CHAPTER IV

THE EXORCISM OF THE GERASENE DEMONIAC

Mark 5:1-20

1. Recovering the Oral Tradition

In this remarkable story, we may trace three
layers of development: a simple exorcism, an elaborated
version and the story as it has been refashioned by
Mark. We shall work from the most recent version to
the earlier ones.

A great choir of scholars has pointed out that
vss. 1-2a and vss. 18-20 exhibit Mark's editorial
creativity.[1] When these accretions are removed, the
story reads thus:

(2b) They met a man out of the tombs with
an unclean spirit, (3) who lived among
the tombs; and no one could bind him any
more, even with a chain; (4) for he had
often been bound with fetters and chains,
but the chains he wrenched apart, and the
fetters he broke in pieces; and no one had
the strength to subdue him. (5) Night and
day among the tombs and on the mountains
he was always crying out, and bruising himself with stones. (6) And when he saw Jesus
from afar, he ran and worshipped him, (7)
and crying out with a loud voice, he said,
"What have you to do with me, Jesus, Son
of the Most High God? I adjure you by God,
do not torment me." (8) For he had said to
him, "Come out of him, you unclean spirit!"
(9) And Jesus asked him, "What is your
name?" He replied, "My name is Legion;
for we are many." (10) And he begged him
eagerly not to send them out of the country. (11) Now a great herd of swine was
feeding on the hillside; (12) and they
begged him, "Send us to the swine, let us

enter them." (13) So he gave them leave,
and the unclean spirits came out, and
entered the swine, and the herd, numbering
about two thousand, rushed down the steep
bank into the sea and were drowned in the
sea. (14) The herdspeople fled and told
it in the city and in the country. And
the people came to see what it was that
had happened. (15) And they came to Jesus
and saw the demoniac sitting there, clothed
and in his right mind, the man who had had
the legion; and they were afraid. (16) And
those who had seen it told what had happened
to the demoniac and to the swine. (17) And
they began to beg Jesus to depart from
their neighborhood.

In this form, some elements disrupt the flow of the
story. These include the detailed description of the
disease (vss. 3-5), the question about the name of the
demon (vs. 9); the plea of the demon for reprieve as
well as the response of the exorcist (vss. 10-13a),
the strange report about the herdspeople (vs. 14) and
their response (vss. 16-17). The fluctuation between
the singular and the plural in reference to the demon
is awkward. We shall see below that these elements
are not merely extraneous decoration but that they
create a level of meaning which is different from both
Mark's use of the story and the life of the story in
its earlier phase.

When these accretions are excised a "typical
exorcism" is left: (1) The presentation of a man with
an unclean spirit, vs. 2b; (2) A defensive reaction on
the part of the demon, vs. 7; (3) The expulsion of the
demon, vs. 8; (4) The departure of the demon from the
man, vs. 13b; (5) The witness of the onlookers, vs.
15.[2] The story, then, would be reconstructed approximately thus:

He met a man out of the tombs who had an
unclean spirit. When the man saw him, he
cried out saying, "What do you have to do
with me, Jesus (?Son of the Most High God?)?
I adjure you, by God, do not torment me."
Jesus said to him, "Come out of the man,
you unclean spirit!" And the unclean
spirit came out. And they saw the demoniac
sitting there, clothed in his right mind,
and they were afraid.[3]

2. Interpretation of the Story

With regard to the first stage of the tradition, we ask, "What human experience is given expression in the portrayal of a man possessed by a demon?" Gerhardus van der Leeuw writes with precision:

> Belief in demons does not mean that chance rules the Universe, but rather that I have experienced the horror of some power which concerns itself neither with my reason nor my morals; and it is not fear of any definite concrete terribleness, but vague tertor of the gruesome and the incomprehensible, which projects itself objectively in belief in demons. Horror, shuddering, sudden fright and the frantic insanity of dread, all receive their form in the demon; this represents the absolute horribleness of the world, the incalcuable force which weaves its web around us and threatens to seize us.[4]

The figure of the demon personifies the intense personal--and sometimes communal--experience of evil. Van der Leeuw points out that such accounts emerge from a variety of diversified backgrounds including texts which influenced Jewis religious thought.

Babylonian texts specifically describe the effects of "the demonic" on human life.

Evil fiends are they!
From the underworld they have gone forth,
They are messengers of Bel, Lord of the World,
The evil spirit that in the desert smiteth
    the living man (sic),
The evil demon that like a cloak enshroudeth
    the man,
The evil ghost, the evil devil that seize upon
    the body,
The hag-demon (and) ghoul that smite the body
    with sickness,
The phantom of the night that in the desert
    roameth abroad,
Unto the wanderer of the night have drawn nigh
Casting a woeful fever upon his body.
A ban of evil hath settled on his body,
An evil disease upon his body they have cast,
An evil plague hath settled on his body.
           (Utukki Limnuti III, 22-45).[6]

The effect of the demons is to challenge the order of the world; the demonic causes the world to seem like a place of chaos.[7] Among the works of the demons are:

> Driving the maiden from your chamber,
> Sending the man forth from his home,
> Expelling the son from the house of his
>   father,
> Hunting the pigeons from their cotes,
> Driving the bird from its nest,
> Making the swallow fly forth from its hole,
> Smiting both oxen and sheep.
> They are evil spirits that chase the great
>   storms,
> Bringing a blight on the land.
>   (IV 28-42)

The demons have unrestricted access to human life: no aspect of experience is immune to evil.

> The highest walls, the thickest walls
> Like a flood they pass.
> From house to house they break through,
> No door can shut them out,
> No bolt can turn them back,
> Through the door like a snake they glide,
> Through the hinge like the wind they blow;
> Estranging the wife from the embrace of a
>   husband,
> Snatching the child from the loins of a man,
> Sending the man forth from his home.
> They are the burning pain
> That bindeth itself upon the back of a man.
>   (V 20-43)

Their influence is thus both cosmic and personal.[8]

A similiar picture is found in popular Greek religion though the elaborate mythological expression is lacking.[9] Egyptian demon-texts are highly developed.[10] Foerster finds many links between the Old Testament and Babylonian belief.[11]

The different strata of the Old Testament are reserved in their attitude toward the demonic. However, echoes are present. The consultation with the witch of Endor is reminiscent of the notion of the spirits of the dead (I Sam. 28:13); The night hag, perhaps a reminiscence of the Babylonian night ghost or storm-spirit of a similar name (Lilitu) is said to find a resting place which shall inhibit her activity

(Is. 13:21; 34:14). Psalm 91:6 may contain a plea for protection against demons of this type. A late text, Tobit 6:8ff., presents a fully developed idea of demons and the demonic.[12]

While linguistic reminiscences in demonology can be noted between Israel and her neighbors, a more important connection is the description of the activity of demon-like beings in the Old Testament. In Isaiah Lilitu dwells in the place of chaos.

> Marmots shall consort with jackals,
> and he-goat shall encounter he-goat,
> There too the night hag shall rest
> and find a place for repose.[13]
> (34:14).

Echoes of the activity of the Canaanite God of plague and pestilence, Resheph, are found in several texts: Deut. 32:24 where the perverse generation is wasted with hunger, overcome by burning heat and overrun by poisonous pestilences; Ps. 78:48 in which cattle are delivered over to hail and thunderbolt; Hab. 3:5 in which pestilence goes before God and plagues follow.[14] In Job 5:7, the Reshpeph seems responsible for trouble from all quarters.[15] In addition, we may note mention of a midday demon (Ps. 91:6) which causes midday sickness. In the same passage, the terror of the night and the catastrophe have linguistic remembrances in mythological, demonic figures.[16]

Deut. 28:22 describes seven evil spirits which will befall the Israelites if they are disobedient: consumption, fever, inflammation, fiery heat, drought, blasting, mildew, perishing. The image of seven evil spirits stretches from Mesopotamia to Jewish apocalyptic. Lev. 16:8, 10, 26 speaks of Azazael, a kind of demon of the desert who receives the scapegoat on the day of atonement. Thus, while Old Testament traditions are reluctant to speak of "the demonic," we find echoes of the intense personal and communal experience of evil which operates independently of moral laws, which inflicts itself on humankind and the description of which has roots deep in human consciousness.

In an extensive investigation of the Hebrew root which translators sometimes render "rebuke" and which the Septuagint and New Testament translate *epitiman*, "rebuke," Howard Clark Kee has traced a line of thought from Ugaritic poems to the New Testament. In the mythology of Ugarit, the good gods rebuke and turn back

49

the powers of chaos. Likewise, in Old Testament texts God rebukes the waters of chaos in a historicization of the mythological battle to which we made reference in our discussion of the stilling of the storm.[17]

Apocalyptic literature is more vivid and definite in its imagery of the demonic. In a prayer, the author of Jubilees prays to be released from the outside forces which bind him/her.

> But do Thou bless me and my sons, that we may increase and multiply and replenish the earth. And Thou knowest how the Watchers, the fathers of these spirits, acted in my day: and as for these spirits which are living, imprison them and hold them fast in the place of condemnation, and let them not bring destruction on the sons of thy servant, my God; for these are malignant, and created in order to destroy.
> (10:5-6)

The age of the power of such unpleasant forces will end when the Messiah breaks the power of Satan and the evil destroyer (23:29).

In Enoch, prayer is made for Azazael in a vision.

> Evil spirits have proceeded from their bodies; because they are born from men (sic) and from the Holy Watchers is their beginning and primal origin. They shall be evil spirits on earth and evil spirits they shall be called. And the spirits of the giants afflict, oppress, destroy, attack, do battle and work destruction on the earth, and cause trouble; they take no food but never-the-less hunger and thirst cause offences. And these spirits shall rise up against the children of men and against the women . . . . (15:9-12)[18]

Enoch wishes to be delivered from the days of slaughter and destruction wrought by the evil spirits.[19]

The Rule of the Qumran community attributes moral lapses to the evil spirit (IQS III 9-11). In the Genesis Apocryphon, we read of an exorcism which is accompanied by prayer and the laying on of hands (IQA 20:28-29).[20] The evil spirits are subjugated as God's reign becomes a reality.[21]

On the first level of the tradition, in Jewish religious life, the story of the possession of the demoniac can be taken not only as a discursive report of a physical possession but as a form which expresses the human experience of being bound by a power outside oneself. The story is a way of describing the personal experience of evil. Indeed, it is as if evil were directed personally at an individual or group. The exorcism is not only a sign of the dawn of the Reign of God but represents the release of the self from outside domination. In the sphere of the power of Jesus, evil loses its control.

The second level of the story is an interpretation in which the demoniac becomes a prototype of the Gentile world and the effect of the coming of the Gospel to that world. This is accomplished by the expansion of vss. 3-6, 10-13, perhaps based on the Septuagint's translation of Ps. 67 and Is. 65.[22]

The lifeline between Isaiah 65 and the pre-Markan pericope is held by the following hooks: Is. 65:4 describes Gentiles who sit in tombs; they eat swine flesh and they spend the night in secret places. In Is. 65:3, the author mentions that Gentiles sacrifice in gardens and burn incense to demons. In 65:7, the location of the abominable acts is the hillside.[23]

Ps. 67 furnishes further points of identification. The demoniac dwells among the tombs as do the Gentiles of Ps. 67:7. The latter are rebellious in the eyes of God and are described as fettered and angry.

In both the Isaianic and the Psalm passages, the images are characterizations of the pitiful condition of the Gentile world. In this sense, the possessed demoniac and the herd of swine may be understood to represent the condition of the Gentile world. The images woven into the story (the tomb, the pigs, self-mutilation, dwelling in darkness) are traditional Jewish images which describe the way Jewish people felt about Gentiles. It is as if the Gentiles have "disorders." Indeed, the description of Gentiles as swine in Jewish circles is attested both in the period of the New Testament (e.g. Enoch 89:12)[24] and much more extensively in the later Rabbinic literature.[25]

If the demoniac is indeed a type of the Gentile world, then we should ask why the swine were destroyed. The usual explanation has been that they demonstrate

51

the reality of the exorcism.[26] But a more subtle
explanation may grow from Isaiah 65. For in that
passage, the Lord is pictured as forsaking those who
forget him. God turns them over to slaughter (vss.
11-12). However, Jesus is able to correct the Gentile disorder and to return the demoniac to his own
people, "clothed and in his right mind." Those who come
into the sphere of Jesus' authority lose their
disorder.

The narrator puts into story form a picture of
the way Jewish hearers imagine their Gentile neigh-
bors--e.g. "living in the tombs." Yet, in the church
the visceral response of Jewish Christians to Gentiles
is relieved. In place of the images of the tomb and
the swine is the image of the demoniac at peace.[27]

At the third level, in characteristic fashion,
Matthew (8:28-34) has greatly reduced the miracle
story to call attention to the dialogue. Jesus has
come to deliver the demons to judgment "before the
time," i.e. prior to the expected apocalyptic
cataclysm.[28] Since the church will later be given the
same authority (10:8), the story is a paradigm for the
ministry of the church.[29]

The story richly illustrates Mark's depiction of
the ministry of Jesus as a battleground between God
and the demons. In addition, Mark uses vss. 19-20
to make the story a statement of the mission to the
Gentiles.[30] The battleground is not simply Israel.
God's victory will include Gentiles.

The third gospel (Luke 8:26-39) lessens the drama
of the exorcism[31] and thus calls attention to the
future ministry of the church among the Gentiles.[32]
The story functions for Luke as a paradigm of the
Gentile mission.

3. The Uses of the Story in Preaching

At the level of the simple exorcism, the two central characters are the demoniac and Jesus. A sermon
could easily follow the outline of their encounter.

We first meet the demoniac. Next, we meet the
healing power in the figure of Jesus. The encounter
between them is initially not pleasant. "What have you
to do with me, Jesus? Do not torment me!" (Perhaps
when one has grown accustomed to it, familiarity is

security even to the possessed). Because the healing power is stronger than the demonic power, the demoniac moves from possession to wholeness.

Demonic possession is the intense personal experience of evil not of one's conscious choosing. Whether personal or social, evil wraps itself in a choke-hold and cripples, maims and robs.

What are some forces and realities in our society, and especially in the life of the preacher's community, which cause us to be like the demoniac? Alcholism? Mental illness? The effect of advertising which causes me to adopt false values? Intense poverty and oppression?

The story of Jesus and the demoniac dramatizes the early church's experience: not only has the power over such restrictive forces been broken, but wholeness is possible. In preaching, if I have used particular images of "possession," can I carry them through to picture the movement from brokenness to wholeness?

This movement, of course, often involves a deep and wrenching struggle between the powers that possess and the healing power. Sometimes it may be a psychological, interior struggle, but other times it may involve conflict between powerful forces in society. At one time, we in the church may find ourselves possessed while at other times we may find ourselves joining in the struggle toward release and wholeness.

At the level of the elaborated version, the demoniac becomes a representative of the Gentile world which, according to traditional Jewish thought, was loathesome and estranged from God. In the church, however, the revulsion of things Gentile has changed. The power of Jesus is enough to transform the intensely negative feeling toward the Gentile world into a picture of health and peace.

At this level it is especially important for the preacher to focus on the life of his or her congregation and community. What values, behaviours, social structures and inner attitudes cause us to regard others as "Gentile?" What causes us to feel about another the way a Jew would have felt seeing the person in the tombs. Or, another approach might seek to identify what causes me to feel as though I am living in the tombs.

53

As in the interpretation of any story, identification is important. It will be one sermon if I identify with the Jewish onlookers who are revulsed by the
demoniac. In that case, the sermon might describe how
my feelings of revulsion can be changed. But if I
identify with the demoniac, then the sermon will follow my own story (and the story of my community) from
dwelling in darkness to the restoration of peace.

A fulcrum on which the sermon turns is the question of how, in the church, under the influence of
the presence of Jesus, are designations like "Gentile"
relativized. How do they lose their negative strength
and how are they replaced by the positive experience
of the man sitting clothed and in his right mind?

NOTES

[1]Dibelius, _Tradition_, p. 74, 87; Nineham, p. 150;
J.F. Craghan, "The Geresene Demoniac," CBQ 30 (1968),
p. 527; R. Pesch, "The Marcan Version of the Healing
of the Geresene Demoniac," _Ecumenical Review_ 23 (1971)
p. 368; A. Fridrichsen, _The Problem of Miracle in
Primitive Christianity_, tr. R. Harrissville and J.
Hanson (Minneapolis: Augsburg, 1972), p. 117; D.
Bartlett, _Exorcism Stories in the Gospel of Mark_,
Unpublished Ph.D. Dissertation, Yale University,
1972, pp. 138-158; R.H. Lightfoot, _History and Inter-
pretation in the Gospels_ (London: Hodder and Stoughton
1935), pp. 88ff., Schweizer, p. 113; T.A. Burkill,
"Concerning Mark 5:7 and Mark 5:18-20," ST 11 (1957),
p. 164, admits the possibility with hesitance; C.H.
Cave, "The Obedience of Unclean Spirits," NTS 11
(1964), p. 95; From a structuralist perspective, see
J. Starbonski, "The Geresene Demoniac: A Literary
Analysis of Mark 5:1-20," _Structural Analysis and Bib-
Lical Exegesis_, tr. A. Johnson and D. Hadidian
(Pittsburg: Pickwick, 1974), p. 60. O. Perels, _Die
Wunderuberlieferung der Synoptiker_ (Berlin-Stuttgart:
Kohlhammer, 1934), pp. 89-90, points out that short
stories tend to be earlier and less styled than
later stories.

[2]Bultmann, HST, p. 210; K. Thraede, "Exorcismus,"
RTHK, vol. 7, pp. 55-63; Craghan, p. 325; Pesch, p.
354.

[3]For a simpler reconstruction, see Cave, pp. 95-
96; for a more complicated reconstruction, see

Craghan, p. 528. For Bartlett's first story, see p. 157. For the main themes in exegesis, see van der Loos, pp. 382ff., and the concise summary in Craghan, pp. 522-524.

[4]Religion in Essence and Manifestation, p. 134. Cf. Otto, The Idea of the Holy, pp. 14-15, 27, 122. M.P. Nilsson, Greek Piety, tr. H. Rose (Oxford: Clarendon, 1948), pp. 60-61; Nilsson, Greek Folk Religion (New York: Harper, 1961) and Nilsson, Geschichte der griesche Religion (Muenchen: Beck, 1950), vol. I;. E. R. Dodds, The Greeks and the Irrational (Berkeley: University of California, 1951).

[5]Van der Leeuw, pp. 138-39, who sees texts describing the demonic having three origins: the experience of nature, dreams and organically caused disease. Van der Loos, p. 339, sees the image of the evil spirit as a personification of fear resulting from a powerful contact with nature, a dream or nightmare, or disease. He compares the possessing effect to that of technology which possesses humankind.

[6]Cited in R. Campbell Thompson, The Devils and Evil Spirits of Babylonia (London: Luzac, 1903), vol. I. Thompson notes the echoes of primitive mythology. On the mythic origins of demons, see the text V 1-43.

[7]On the theme of chaos-order in the demonic, see F.J. Leenhardt, "An Exegetical Essay on Mark 5:1-20," Structural Analysis and Biblical Exegesis, tr. A. Johnson and D. Hadidean (Pittsburgh: Pickwick, 1974), p. 103 and Starbonski, pp. 70-71.

[8]In equally experiential terms, Cumont writes of the demonic in Persian religion: " . . . both violent and cunning, impetuous and crafty, they were the authors of all the calamities that befell the world, such as pestilence, famine, tempests and earthquakes. They kindled evil passions and illicit desires in the hearts of men (sic) and provoked war and sedition. They were clever deceivers rejoicing in lies and impostures. They encouraged the phantasmagoria and mystification of the sorcerers. . ." F. Cumont, Oriental Religions in Roman Paganism (New York: Dover, 1956), p. 153; cf. p. 266, n. 37-40.

[9]W. Foerster, "daimon," TDNT. Vol. II, pp. 6-8; van der Loos, p. 341.

[10]Van der Loos, p. 341.

[11]Foerster, p. 15.

[12]In order not to press the Old Testament for more than can be fairly claimed, I have taken a conservative view. An extensive bibliography is given in T.H. Gaster, "Demons," IDB, vol. I, pp. 823-24 and updated by J. Hull, "Demons in the NT," IDB, Supplementary Volume, p. 225 and Hull, "Exorcism in the NT," IDB, Supplementary Volume, p. 314.

[13]On Lilitu, the night hag, see Gaster, pp. 818-819. Mesopotamian texts attest a similar figure as a sexual temptress in dreams.

[14]Amen Hotep II claims that he strides across a stream with the fury of a Rasap.

[15]Gaster, p. 819.

[16]Ibid., p. 820.

[17]H.C. Kee, "The Terminology of Mark's Exorcism Stories," NTS 14 (1968), pp. 131-149.

[18]Enoch presents the demons as apostate angels whose disobedience forbade them entrance to the courts of heaven and whose ultimate end will be destruction by fire. Qumran and the Testaments see the demonic as a force opposed to God. Ecclesiasticus calls the demonic "agents of vengeance" sent by God.

[19]Foerster, p. 15.

[20]Kee, pp. 233-34.

[21]Rabbinic texts later than the NT have stories which describe mad people in terms very similar to our pericope. See esp. bNidda 17a; Strack-Billerbeck, Vol. I, p. 491; Foerster, pp. 13-14 and Fiebig, Juedische Wundergeschichten.

[22]This has been noticed by Pesch, p. 371; Craghan, p. 529; Nineham, p. 151; Schweizer, p. 113; Cave, p. 75; Sahlin, "Die Perikope vom gerasenischer Beseener und der plan des Markusevangeliums," ST 18 (1964), pp. 159-72, who describes the pericope as a Christian midrash in which the possessed person is a symbol of the pagans as a whole (p. 160).

[23]Paul draws on Isaiah 65 when discussing the question of Jews and Gentiles, Romans 10:21.

[24]Cf. 89:42 where boars devour sheep until the Lord of the sheep comes. In 89:72, wild boars are equated with Samaritans.

[25]See bSan 93a. Cave, p. 97, cites Ber R 63:8. Cf. the title of Strack-Billerbeck's paragraph on this theme, vol. I, p. 449.

[26]Craghan, p. 531.

[27]Leenhardt points out that a first century person who heard the story might have seen himself/herself as the demoniac whose brokenness would be restored (p. 88).

[28]Held, p. 174, 244ff; Fenton, pp. 131-33; P. Ellis, p. 43-44; Waetjen, pp. 121-22; Gundry, pp. 159-160; Schweizer, Matthew, p. 223.

[29]Held, p. 245, points out that 8:29 places the story in the service of Christology. For Matt., the mission of Jesus is also the mission of the church.

[30]E.g., Nineham, p. 155; Schweizer, Mark, p. 114; S.E. Johnson, The Gospel According to St. Mark, HNTC (New York: Harper, 1960), p. 103; V. Taylor, The Gospel According to St. Mark (London: Macmillan, 1966), pp. 284-85; Cf. O. Bauernfiend, Die Worte der Daemonen im Markusevangelium (Stuttgart, 1927).

[31]Achtemeier, "The Lukan Perspective," p. 163, following Bauernfiend, pp. 100-101.

[32]Marshall, p. 335; Fitzmyer, p. 735 who describes "sitting at the feet of Jesus" (8:35, 10:39, Acts 22:3) as a Lukan picture of discipleship; E. Ellis, p. 131.

CHAPTER V

THE WOMAN WITH THE ISSUE OF BLOOD

Mark 5:24b-34

1. Recovering the Oral Tradition

While vs. 24b may be Mark's reworking of an existing editorial seam, the pericope is basically pre-markan.[1]

2. Interpretation of the Story

Most discussion of this story has centered around exegetical details,[2] such as the type of medical disorder it may have been, the tassels on the garment. In addition, the story can be placed in a larger framework: the nature of uncleanliness and the church's experience of the lifting of that onus.[3]

Many commentators call attention to the fact that a woman with an irregular issue of blood was regarded as unclean. Lev. 15:25-27 describes her situation.

> When a woman has a prolonged discharge of blood not at the time of her menstruation, or when her discharge continues beyond the period of her menstruation, her impurity shall last all the time of her discharge; she shall be unclean as during the period of her menstruation. Any bed on which she lies during the time of her discharge shall be like that which she used during menstruation, and everything on which she sits shall be unclean as in her menstrual uncleanness. Every person who touches them shall be unclean . . . .[4]

Hauck and Grundmann stress that in the period of the New Testament, not only is the woman with the issue of blood ritually unclean, she is socially unacceptable.[5]

Indeed, wherever the woman sleeps, walks or sits is counted as unclean and any person who comes into physical contact with those things is declared unclean and must undergo ritual purification. If the woman's bleeding stopped, she could be purified and thus socially recycled (Lev. 15:25-30). The specific issue is the flow of blood, but the larger issue is uncleanliness and its isolating personal and social consequences.

Ethnographic literature does not make clear _why_ the early connection was drawn between the discharge of blood, or indeed between the many discharges issuing from the body--e.g. semen, excretion--and uncleanliness.[6] With varying degrees of severity, many cultures from earliest recorded time, reflect the taboo of women who are in the menstrual cycle and, therefore, issuing blood. In some primitive cultures, not only is that which the affected person touched declared unclean, but those who look upon such persons are ruled unclean. This sometimes led to the seclusion of women from society.[7] In other cultures, contact with blood itself led to uncleanliness.[8]

Rudolf Otto describes the phenomenon.

> The unclean is loathsome, that which stirs strong feelings of natural disgust. And it is just during the more primitive stages of human development that the emotion of disgust exercises special power. Probably these reactions are a part of our natural self-protective endowment, instinctive safeguards for many important, vital functions. The effect of civilization is to refine these emotions of disgust and loathing by diverting them to different objects, so that things which were loathsome to the savage cease to be so and things which were not become so.[9]

Otto finds that the experience of disgust is a deep response which wells up from the recesses of human consciousness. The reason for the revulsion is not always rational, but the experience is powerful and the effect is abiding. In the course of the development of civilization, the rational and the emotive are sometimes integrated, as law develops, and the disgust is clearly identified. Says Otto, "We have ourselves a direct experience of the same thing today in our emotional reaction to the sight of flowing blood which it would be hard to say whether the element of 'disgust' or 'horror' is the stronger."[10] In the larger context, uncleanness can be brought about by eating, by actions, by bodily functions as well as by a host of other causes.

Thus, we should expect religious language at the time of the New Testament to reflect the sense of revulsion over the issue of blood and uncleanliness. The Zadokite fragment uses the analogy of the "ways of an unclean woman" to describe the effect of transgression (5:4). The earth itself is made unclean when blood is shed on it through killing (Jubilees 7:24ff.). The person who eats blood, i.e. nonkosher, is to be rooted out of the land (6:11). Those who eat blood are the unclean Gentiles (Enoch 98:11), and the woman who is menstruating is defiled and unclean (15:4).

Rabbinic documents assembled after the close of the New Testament are even more stringent. One whole tractate of the Mishnah, Zabim, is devoted to the problem. The person who touches the victim of the flowing blood is unclean. Likewise, uncleanness is generated by touching anything used by the unclean person.[11] The Talumud's commentary on Zabim does nothing more than reproduce the text of the tractate; no exegesis was needed.[12] Thus, the experience of uncleanness was very much alive in the Palestinian world.

The picture of the woman with the flow of blood is desperate. She has been seeking relief for twelve years. Without the cessation of the flow of blood, she has no chance of becoming clean and thereby being restored to her proper religious and social spheres. When she is made well, the healing is a transmutation to cleanliness and social acceptability. The medium of cleansing is faith.

In Jewish religious literature of the period, as far as I can tell, there are no instances in which faith refers to miraculous events.[13] While having many accents, the leading theme is that of one's orientation to God. For Enoch, those whose faith is not in God dwell in the midst of darkness and sickness (46:1-8). In contrast, the righteous are those who live in the heritage of faith and who will have unending days of life (58:1-5; 68:1-5). In IV Ezra, faith places one among those who will be resurrected (7:34). Faith provides one with an avenue of escape from the last days. This is true for those who

61

recognize God's revelation during their own lifetimes (9:7; 13:22). "Faithfulness shall flourish." (6:27). II Baruch thinks that faith gives God an opportunity to reveal the secrets of the coming Messianic reign (54:5). The reign is the obverse of the broken character life which was established with Adam (compare 56:6 and 73). Faith is not trust in the miraculous manipulation of nature but in the providential care of God.

While the verb "to save" can refer strictly to the healing of the body and to deliverance from impending doom, W. Foerster has shown that in religious literature of the period, the concept of salvation takes on many nuances of meaning which have to do with the deliverance of the righteous from the miseries of life. When one speaks of "being saved" in first century Jewish circles, one speaks of restoration of broken selves and restoration of the broken world. The time reference to the period of salvation is not exclusively to the last period.[14]

That this is the meaning intended in the present pericope is suggested in two ways. First, the book of Enoch confirms that the Messianic era will include the end of uncleanness (10:20-22). The Lord wills for the unclean to be made clean in the last day (T. Jos. 4:6). The Qumran community enacted this idea with ritual lustrations. Secondly, peace was expected to overflow in the time of deliverance, e.g. Enoch 5:9; 10:17; 11:12; 58:4; 71:15, 17; 92. Indeed, in the time of salvation, Enoch says, "And their lives shall be increased in peace" (5:9).

The wholeness and peace which is indicated by "salvation" can be appropriated by faith. Faith, indeed, is to flourish in that time and faith transfers one to the realm of the saved (IV Ezra 6:25-29; 9: 7-8).

In this story, one who has suffered under the onus of uncleanliness has been released. Peace has come.[15] Those who hear the story can have the same experience.[16] The story projects into narrative form the feeling of what it is to have a feeling of uncleanness lifted. The agency is the orb of the authority of Jesus.

For Matthew (9:20-23), the miracle is clearly secondary to the narrative teaching about faith: everything that does not support the role of faith is removed. The healing itself becomes an illustration of

the saying, "Your faith has saved you."[17] The story
is a paradigm for the church.

In addition to illustrating the conflict between
God and disease, the story in Mark illustrates the
faith necessary for Jairus in the next incident. When
the latter came to Jesus, his daughter was alive.
Jesus' journey to the home of the ruler was interrupted
by the healing of the woman. When the report came to
Jesus and Jairus that the child was dead, Jairus had a
background from which to understand Jesus' remark, "Do
not fear, only believe." Although the church lived
(and lives) in the battleground of the world, the power
which defeated Satan in the ministry of Jesus may be
appropriated by faith.[18]

Luke (8:42-48) characteristically foregoes detail
regarding the woman and devalues the role of faith by
heightening the description of the miracle itself and
its effect on the woman. The saying about faith is
little more than tacked onto the end of the story.[19]
The emphasis is on the power which went forth from Jesus, and like other miracle stories, this one illustrates the power which will be given to the church.

3. The Use of the Story in Preaching

The woman's medical problem is not a particularly
troubling one today. A blood coagulant or perhaps a
surgical procedure could correct the malfunction.

However, the feeling which comes to expression in
the character of the woman is that of uncleanness and
its subsequent social consequence, aloneness. If the
preacher identifies with the woman, he or she may want
to locate experiences or situations which, like the
uncontrolled flow of blood, arouse in us the feeling
of being unclean, unacceptable, almost untouchable and
consequently isolated and alone.

In the ancient world, the fear of uncleanness
lead to sanctions against those who were unclean. Our
culture practices quarantine only in a few cases of
infectious disease, and these generally lack the revulsion aroused by the sight of an unclean person in
the first century. Nonetheless, nearly every ethnic
or economic group regards some conditions or behavior
in much the same way that uncleanness was regarded in
early first century Palestine.

In suburbia, my spouse and I knew a family whose life appeared to be taken out of the pages of Better Homes and Gardens. But the marriage was falling apart. When the news became public, the woman said she felt like a quarantine sign had been placed on their lot. What happens to a junior high girl who becomes pregnant, or to a man in his prime who is diagnosed with inoperable cancer? What does it do to a Hispanic in a crowded elevator to feel someone consciously edge away?

Our culture is fascinated with beautiful bodies. Make-up, orthodontic "correction," contact lenses, health spas--all serve to make our bodies more attractive. What happens to our self-image, our sense of self-worth, when we no longer look like we have just stepped out of a television commercial for Estee' Lauder?

The woman did not approach Jesus directly. Instead she used the crowd as a cover while she came up behind him. Why would an unclean person take such an indirect approach? How can someone in our culture express their longing to be made clean and to be accepted in such an indirect way?

The woman reached out and touched Jesus' garment. We have no physical cloth to touch, but perhaps the community of faith can provide the life and fellowship which results in the unacceptable being made to feel acceptable. Or if the church is so strangled by cultural mores that it causes people to feel unclean and unacceptable, perhaps the preacher can point to other forces and realities in which a person unclean and alone can find cleanliness and community.

In preaching, then, we may want to provide an experience of the imagination which will encourage a person who feels unclean and alone to sense what it is like to feel clean and part of a community.

NOTES

[1] Rebecca Patten, pp. 87-88.

[2] Van der Loos offers a comprehensive discussion of theories about the nature of the flow of blood. Most of the opinions favor chronic hemorrhage connected with the menstrual cycle (pp. 509ff.). A. Richardson,

The Miracle Stories of the Gospels (London: SCM, 1941), suggests (without evidence) that the Biblical notion of the connection of sin and sickness underlies the story (p. 62).

[3]Except for the emphasis on faith and the conclusion in vs. 34, the story is a typical healing. Bultmann, HST, p. 215; Klostermann, p. 51; Weinrich, _Antike Heilungswunder_, pp. 63ff., Strack-Billerbeck, Vol. I, p. 520.

[4]Lev. 21:1-5 indicates that a woman was unclean at the time of childbirth and Lev. 15:19-24 underscores the uncleanliness connected with the menstrual cycle.

[5]Hauck, p. 69; Grundmann, p. 114. On the problem of the social consequences of defilement, see M. Douglas, _Purity and Danger_ (New York: Prueger, 1966), pp. 41ff. and _idem_, _Natural Symbols_ (New York: Pantheon 1970) as well as the general discussion in B. Malina, _The New Testament World_ (Atlanta: John Knox, 1981), pp. 122-154.

[6]L. Tombs, for example, describes it as an "irrational revulsion," "Clean and Unclean," IDB, vol. I, p. 644. H. Robinson says that blood, especially women's blood, is regarded as mysterious and potent and he calls attention to the "wide-spread tabu" associated with blood, "Blood," ERE, vol. II, pp. 714-719. Cf. W. Muhlmann, "Blut," RGG, vol. I, pp. 1327-28. F. Hauck notes that uncleanliness is a power, "akatharos," TDNT, Vol. III, p. 416. Cf. van der Leeuw, vol. I, p. 43.

[7]See the evidence in J. Frazer, _The Golden Bough_ (New York: Macmillan, 1935), vol. III, pp. 145-46; vol. X, pp. 22-100. One can appreciate Frazer's collection of data without appropriating his interpretation. For critique, see Douglas, _Purity and Danger_, passim.

[8]Ibid., vol. III, pp. 239-252; pp. 250-51 describe the fear of a man passing under the blood of a living woman.

[9]Otto, p. 122.

[10]Ibid., p. 123.

[11]_The Mishnah_, tr. H. Danby (Oxford: Clarendon, 1933). Cf. Strack-Billerbeck, vol. I, p. 520.

[12]See S. Lehman, "Introduction to tractate Zabim" in _The Babylonian Talmud_, ed. I. Epstein (London: Soncino, 1935ff.), vol. VI, pt. 2, p. 501. For passages discussing defilement by blood, see bHul 33a, 72a, 84b, 87b, 127b; bNazir 38a, 49b, 54a, 57a; bSan 72a, 72b, and esp. bMeg 28b; bBm 84b; bHor 3b, 4a.

[13]W. Foerster, "_sodzo_," TDNT, Vol. VII, pp. 980-986.

[14]_Ibid_.

[15]In this context, peace refers to much more than "inner peace;" it refers to the cessation of intra-personal and interpersonal conflict and to the positive growth of the community.

[16]Schweizer, _Mark_, p. 120; Fuller, p. 86; Richardson, p. 61; Nineham, p. 159. All see the _Sitz-im-Leben_ as the preaching of the church in which the story was expected to arouse faith.

[17]Held, pp. 178-79, 215ff., 240; Schweizer, _Matthew_, p. 229; P. Ellis, p. 148; Waetjen, pp. 125-26; Kingsbury, pp. 568ff.; contra Gundry, p. 174.

[18]The centrality of faith is emphasized by Nineham, p. 158; Johnson, p. 107; Robinson, p. 73; Taylor, p. 293; Schweizer, _Mark_, p. 118.

[19]Held, p. 218; Achtemeier, "The Lukan Perspective" (on power), p. 158; Marshall, p. 345.

CHAPTER VI

THE RAISING OF JAIRUS' DAUGHTER

Mark 5:22-23, 35-42

1. Recovering the Oral Tradition

Clearly the story of the raising of Jairus' daughter has been interrupted by the story of the woman with the issue of blood (5:25b-34).[1] While this insertion may have taken place before Mark made use of the two stories, Mark has edited the seam in vs. 21 and added vs. 43.[2] The name Jairus was likely added prior to Mark but may not have belonged to the incipient form of the story.[3] The paramater of the story is vss. 22-24, 35-42.

> (22) Then came one of the rulers of the synongogue, Jairus by name, and seeing him he fell at his feet, (23) and he sought him saying, "My little daughter is at the point of death. Come and lay hands on her so that she may be made well, and live." (24) And he went with him. (35) And while they were still (?walking?), there came some from the ruler's house who said, "Your daughter is dead, why trouble the Teacher any further?" (36) But ignoring what they said, Jesus said to the ruler of the synongogue, "Do not fear; only believe." (37) And he allowed no one to follow him (?except Peter, James and John, the brother of James?). (38) When they came to the house of the ruler of the synongogue, he saw a tumult, and people weeping and wailing loudly, (39) and when he had entered he said to them, "Why do you make a tumult and weep? The child is not dead but sleeping." (40) And they laughed at him. But he put them all outside, and took the child's father and mother and those who were with him

67

and went in where the child was. (41)
Taking her by the hand, he said to her,
"Talitha cumi," which means, "Little girl,
I say to you, arise." (42) And immediately
the girl got up and walked; for she was
twelve years old. And they were overcome
with amazement.

2. Interpretation of the Story

Even the better commentaries tend to focus on the
lexical details of this story rather than on the story
as a whole.[4] The most common unifying motif discussed
by expositors is the notion of the raising of the dead
being an anticipation of the final reign of God. The
narrative witnesses to the church's experience of release from the fear of the dreaded power of death.

Without intending to claim a line of historical
development from the myth to the story of the raising
of Jairus' daughter, we may again turn to the Akkadian
saga of Gilgamesh for a mythic portrayal of human
feeling about death. Gilgamesh and Enkidu have retired
for the night when Enkidu has a dream in which the
council of gods meets and decides that Enkidu's fate
is death. Their mutual sorrow is poignant.

Enkidu lay down (ill) before Gilgamesh.
And as his tears were streaming down,
(he said):
"O my brother, my dear brother! Me they
would
Clear at the expense of my brother!"
Furthermore:
"Must I by the spirit of the dead
Sit down at the spirit's door,
Never again (to behold) my dear brother
(with mine) eyes?" (VII 2:16-23)

The response of Gilgamesh to Enkidu's death is trau-
matic.

Hear me, O Elders, (and give ear) unto me!
It is for Enkidu, my (friend) that I weep,
Moaning bitterly like a wailing woman.
The axe at my side, my hand's trust,
The drik in my belt, (the shield) in front
of me,
My festal robe, my richest trimming--
An evil demon rose up and robbed me!

                . . .
        What now is this sleep that has laid hold
            on thee?
        Thou art benighted and canst not hear (me)!
        But he lifts not up (his eyes).
                        (VIII 2:1-8, 12-13)

Gilgamesh tears off his clothing and throws it to the
ground and weeps.

        For Enkidu, his friend, Gilgamesh
        Weeps bitterly as he ranges over the steppe:
        "When I die shall I not be like Enkidu?
        Woe has entered my belly.
        Fearing death I roam over the steppe."
                        (IX 1:1-5)

Although the death of Enkidu is willed by the council
of the gods, Gilgamesh is terrified by death. He is
reluctant to accept death as the final curtain on the
human drama. Consequently, he goes in search of immortality and rebels against the fate of Enkidu. In
his journey he meets with Shamash and they converse in
graphic idiom.

        "Gilgamesh, whither rovest thou?
        The life thou pursuest thou shalt not find."
        Gilgamesh says to him, to valiant Shamash:
        "After marching (and) roving over the steppe,
        Must I lay my head in the heart of the earth
        That I may sleep through all the years?
        Let mine eyes behold the sun
            That I may have my fill of the light!
        Darkness withdraws when there is enough light.
        May one who indeed is dead behold yet the
            radiance of the sun." (X 1:7-16).

        Utnapishtim, one who has attained everlasting
life by navigating a terrible flood, tells Gilgamesh
of a city where the traveller might find immortality.
Yet when Gilgamesh arrives, everlasting life is not to
be his. The verdict on Gilgamesh, the lonely traveller, is to go to the netherworld. Once in the netherworld, he meets Enkidu. But their reunion is scarcely
joyful.

        "Tell me, my friend, tell me, my friend,
        Tell me the order of the nether world which
            thou hast seen."
        "I shall not tell thee! I shall not tell
            thee!

                        69

But if I tell thee the order of the nether
  world which I have seen,
Sit thou down and weep!"
" (. . .) I will sit down and weep."
"(My body . . . , which thou didst touch
  as thy heart rejoiced,
Vermin devour (as though) an old garment.
(My body . . .) which thou didst touch
  as thy heart rejoiced,
(. . .) is filled with dust."
He cried "(Woe!)" and threw himself (in the
  dust). (XII 87-100)

This long story reveals ancient feeling toward the
fate of humankind.

Similar echoes come to expression in various
strands of the Old Testament. Death is the irrevocable
fact of human existence (Ps. 78:50; 89:48). It causes
writers to be in distress (18:4), to be terrified
(55:4), to feel ensnared or trapped (116:3). Such is
the feeling that when the body is taken from the bier
and placed in a pit with the bones of other corpses,
the act is regarded, in some circles, as surrendering
that person's individuality.[5]

The abode of the dead, a place of unlimited,
cheerless residence, is a place to be dreaded and
feared. Indeed, people cry out for deliverance from
death (Pss. 6:5; 28:1; 30:1; 88:12; 115:17).[6] Death
can almost be personified as one who seizes human
beings (Ps. 55:15).[7] The dead cannot praise God and
are cut off from communion and fellowship with God
(Ps. 88:5; Is. 38:18). In a graphic image which is
reproduced in Mk. 5:39, the dead are said to be
asleep (Job 14:10-12; Ps. 3:5; 4:8; 13:3). In death,
not only are people cut off from life, but they are
cut off from God, the source of life.

Like Gilgamesh, the longing for this power to be
broken found expression in pre-apocalyptic texts.
Isaiah and Zechariah, for instance, look forward to the
day when children shall live to be a hundred years
old and when women and men shall live out their days to
the full (Is. 65:20; Zech. 8:4). Psalms voice the hope
that God will not abandon human beings to oblivion forever (Pss. 16:9; 49:16; 73:23). In Isaiah's "little
apocalypse," God is said to wipe away every tear and to
swallow up death (25:8). Daniel speaks of those who
are asleep but who will rise to everlasting life--or to
everlasting condemnation (12:2). Indeed, says Isaiah,

They that sleep in the earth will awake
   and shout for joy,
      for thy dew is a dew of sparkling light,
   and the earth will bring those long dead to
      birth again (26:19).[8]

When the Lord comes, the light of life will overcome
the shadows of death.

In apocalyptic literature, death is regarded as
an aberration of human life and as an enemy.[9] Even
the righteous will die (e.g. IV Ezra 7:21, 8:31; Enoch
102:10ff.). However, apocalyptic authors voice the
conviction that the dead are "asleep in hope" (e.g.
II Baruch 30:2; Enoch 100:5). Enoch envisions a temporary Messianic rule during which the dead sleep and
toward the end of which they come back to life.

The resurrection which appears in apocalyptic
texts is somewhat different from the raising of Jairus'
daughter. For apocalyptic literature does not see
merely a return to physical existence but a time in
which the dead are made alive as a time when "the evil
root is sealed up" and "death is hidden" (IV Ezra
8:43). The dead do not, like Jairus' daughter, arise
to die again.

Many passages in which authors anticipate resurrection also anticipate the restitution of other broken
aspects of life. For example, consider the picture in
T. Judah.

And he shall be the people of the Lord, and
   have one tongue
And there shall be no spirit of deceit
   (Belair),
For he shall be cast into the fire forever.
And they who have died in grief shall arise
   in joy,
And they who were poor for the Lord's sake
   shall be made rich,
And they who are put to death for the Lord's
   sake shall awake to life.
And the harts of Jacob shall run in
   joyfulness,
And the eagles of Israel shall fly in
   gladness;
And all people shall glorify the earth
   forever (25:3-5).

At the same time that the dead are raised, Enoch sees
a great cosmic transformation.

> And in those days shall the mountains leap
>   like rams,
> And the hills also shall skip like lambs
>   satisfied with milk,
> And the faces of all the angels in heaven
>   shall be lighted up with joy.
>
> And the earth shall rejoice,
> And the righteous shall dwell upon it,
> And the elect shall walk thereon. (51:4-5)
>
> And then there shall be bestowed upon
>   the elect wisdom,
> And they shall all live and never again sin,
> Either through ungodliness or through pride;
> But they who are wise shall be humble.
>
> And they shall not again transgress,
> Nor shall they sin all the days of their
>   life,
> Nor shall they die of divine anger or wrath,
> But they shall complete the number of the
>   days of their life.
>
> And their lives shall be increased in peace,
> And the years of their joy shall be multi-
>   plied,
> In eternal gladness and peace,
> All the days of their life. (5:9).

When the resurrection comes, the terror of death will
be put away and a time of wholeness of life will
dawn.[10] The apocalyptic texts are word-pictures of the
way the writers feel about death and their longing
for life.

These powerful associations may be the reason
that "death" is frequently used in a transferred sense
to describe the quality of life apart from God.   The
Deuteronomist, for instance, contrasts participation
in the covenant with the lack of participation by use
of the figures of life and death.

> See, I have set before you this day life
> and good, death and evil. If you obey
> the commandment of the Lord . . . then
> you shall live and multiply. But if your
> heart turns away and you will not hear

> . . . you shall perish . . . I have set
> before you life and death, blessing and
> curse. Therefore, choose life.
> (30:15-19, passim)

Writing of the plight of the ungodly, the author of the
Wisdom of Solomon says, "So we also, as soon as we were
born, ceased to be" (5:13). The ungodly are "spiritually dead." Thus Walter Brueggemann notes that
death can be used "symbolically, as the loss of rich,
joyous existence as willed by God. Thus 'life' refers
to total well being, and death is the loss of total
well being."[11]

The feeling which comes to expression in the story
of the raising of Jairus' daughter is the heartbreaking
fear of death and the experience of the early church
that that fear is now ended. In its faith, the church
encountered a power stronger than death.[12]

One clue by which we may understand the use of the
story in the early church is 5:36: "Do not fear, only
believe." In a missionary situation, or in the
preaching and teaching of the church for itself, these
words are directed not only to Jairus but to the
hearer of the story. In apocalyptic texts, we noted
that only the righteous are raised to life: the un-
righteous are raised to contempt and unhappiness.
Faith transfers one to the realm of the righteous
(Enoch 39:6; 58:5; II Baruch 54:21) and, therefore, can
release one's fear of death. Faith makes salvation
possible (IV Ezra 6:25ff., 7:26; 9:7-9) and "though the
righteous sleep a long sleep, they have nought to
fear" (Enoch 100:5).[13]

Once again Matthew (9:18-19, 23-25) has abbre-
viated the story by eliminating details of the miracle
itself. This casts into centerstage the conversation
between Jesus and the now unnamed ruler which concerns
faith. The ruler's faith thereby becomes a paradigm
for the church (10:8).[14]

In Mark, the central opposition of the story is
between Jesus and the power of death. As the story
opened, it appeared that Jesus would be needed only for
a conventional healing because (unlike Matthew's report) the girl was near death but still alive. The
story shows convincingly that God is stronger than
death. Coming as it does at the climax of the four-
story cycle, the story foreshadows the dramatic victory

over death which God will win at the resurrection.[15]
A share in that victory is granted by faith.

Luke's editing of the story is restricted to
ironing out some of the crinkles in the narrative.[16]
Of the first three gospels, Luke gives the story its
most dramatic setting (8:40-42, 49-56). For it comes
as the climax of four miracle stories which illustrate
the power and authority of Jesus as well as what it
means to bring the good news of the reign of God. The
story is followed immediately (9:1-2) by the giving of
power and authority to the twelve for the purpose of
preaching, healing and bringing the good news of the
reign of God. It is thus an illustration of the
authority which will later belong to the church (e.g.
Acts 9:36-42).

3. The Use of the Story in Preaching

Distinct homiletical doors are opened by different
perspectives on the story. The keys are the ways in
which we understand the meaning of the theme of death
and the characters with which we identify.

We may treat the theme of death as a metaphor for
the strangling restriction which takes hold of some
persons and situations. In the story, death is not
simply a result of a chain of physical events but is a
power which attempts to crush the spark and sparkle of
life.

Persons and situations may not lose their existence but, instead, lose their purpose, meaning and
sense of power. Numb to life, they are the living
dead. Our culture provides an abundance of symbols
which bespeak the living death, from the hollow-eyed
youth in the ghetto to suburbanites endlessly looking
for the new and different to the nuclear missile
sitting silently in its silo.

The daughter, then, may be a figure for such
death. She was at home, growing ever more still, cold
and clammy. Is there a better representation of some
of the movements in our culture--and in our churches?
And, if left to pursue its own course, unchallenged,
this dry-rot can result in physical death as in sui-
cide or nuclear holocaust.

The story opens with the picture of the desperate Jairus. On one level his desperation is not for himself but for his daughter. And yet, when someone close to us is threatened, we feel threatened ourselves. The death, or impending death, of one close to us reminds us of our own fragility. In what situations are we like Jairus--confronted by the power of death but desperate to avoid it? Perhaps we can identify some forces and trends, social and personal, which cause us to feel like Jairus.

Jairus turns to Jesus for help. The ruler believes that the power of Jesus is stronger than the power of death. Sometimes we encounter the power dramatized by the figure of Jesus in the church, but sometimes the church itself is an agent of the living death, especially when it (we) co-operates with, and even blesses, events, trends and forces which shackle, manipulate and exclude. Sometimes, then, we encounter the power of new life in altogether surprising places and groups--as surprising in our day as Jesus was in his.

Nonetheless, despite the presence of the one who can bring life out of death, those who come from the home of the ruler bring word that it is too late. The little girl has died. All that remains is to bury the corpse; the messengers and mourners have capitulated to the power of death. Indeed, the mourners even make a living from death! In a perverse way, the coming of a power stronger than death does not seem like altogether good news to them.

In the final scene, Jesus brings the little girl back to life. This pictures the experience of the church: the enemy, death, has been subdued by a stronger power.

While the physical presence of Jesus is no longer available to take us by the hand, the story of the resurrection of Jesus affirms that God is still able to bring life from death. As we live in the orb of the values and presence of Jesus, life returns.

The story also provides an opportunity for us to reflect on our own attitudes and feelings toward physical death in light of the experience of the church as expressed in the story. The last decade has produced an abundance of literature, provacative and insightful, but there is no substitute for coming face to face with our own fears and hopes.

When thinking about the death of one close to us, or perhaps about our own death, how are we like Jairus? The figures of the mourners present an occasion on which to think about our own culture's funeral practices as well as our attitude about the finality of death. The final scene, however, pictures the experience of the church: in the presence of Jesus life has the last word.

NOTES

[1]The story of the woman with the issue of blood and the story of the raising of Jairus' daughter were not originally from one hand. The style of Greek in the former is noticeably better than in the latter (see the commentaries ad loc. and Bultmann, HST, p. 214). A more difficult question is whether they were joined together in the pre-Markan tradition or by Mark. Authorities are divided. Each story could have circulated independently since there is no reason for them to have circulated together and since "sandwiching" is a characteristic of Markan style. However, the reliable Paul Achtemeier gives convincing reasons why they might have been joined in the pre-Markan period, "Toward the Isolation of the Pre-Marcan Miracle Catenae," JBL 89 (1970), p. 278. Cf. H.C. Kee, Community of the New Age (Philadelphia: Westminster, 1977), pp. 32-33.

[2]A summary of research is given in Rebecca Patten, pp. 25-87, Pryke, p. 14. Some interpreters find additional Markan activity in 41b (the explanation, "which means" etc.) and in 42b (the cry of amazement).

[3]See, e.g. the question of whether the name was originally part of the story. Hauck thinks it is a play on words since the root means "to awaken" (p. 38). However, it is the daughter who is awakened. Most scholars follow Bultmann in thinking the name is secondary (HST, p. 215). For more recent assessment, see Pesch, "Jairus," BibZ 14 (1970), pp. 225-26.

[4]Thus Van der Loos speaks of the whole discussion being under a "cloud of stipulations," (p. 572).

[5]R. Bultmann, "zao," TDNT, Vol. II, p. 846.

[6]Another tradition seems to regard death as the end of all existence, II Sam. 14:4; Job 7:21; Ps. 39:13.

[7]In Ugaritic texts, Sheol and Mot act as agents of death, thereby personifying death as an enemy.

[8]Is it accidental that one of the primary images for life in the epic of Gilgamesh turns up in Isaiah, albeit without literary dependence?

[9]Death comes unnaturally through Eve (II Enoch 30:18) or through sin (Enoch 69:11), through Adam (II Barch 23:4) or through the devil (Wisdom 2:24). On the whole discussion, see the comprehensive work of G. Nickelsburg, Jr., Resurrection, Immortality and Eternal Life in Intertestamental Judaism (Cambridge: Harvard, 1972).

[10]On different expectations in the period, see Bultmann, "zao," pp. 855-859 and W. Bousett, Die Religion des Judentums im spaethellenistischen Zeitalter, ed. H. Gressman (Tuebingen: Mohr, 1966), pp. 275-79.

[11]W. Brueggemann, "Death, Theology of," IDB Supplementary Volume, p. 220. Cf. the excellent discussion of L. Bailey, Sr., Biblical Perspectives on Death (Philadelphia: Fortress, 1979), pp. 40-41, who notes that death is used "to describe various conditions which detract from the full potential which Yahweh intended for his (sic) creatures; it is used as a value judgment on the quality of life so that a weak and ineffective person, a 'nobody,' can be called a 'dead dog,' (I Sam. 24:14)."

[12]A host of smaller exegetical problems are discussed in the commentaries.

[13]As far as I can tell, in apocalyptic writings faith does not refer to faith in the Messianic figure but to trust in God. The triumph of faith and the resurrection of the dead are brought into mutual association in IV Ezra 7:35-57; 9:7; Enoch 61:4-5; II Baruch 54:21.

[14]Held, pp. 178-80; Schweizer, Matthew, p. 229; P. Ellis, p. 148; Kingsbury, p. 568ff.

[15]For Mark, death is the work of Satan, Hamilton, p. 85.

[16]Achtemeier, "The Lukan Perspective," p. 155; Fitzmyer, p. 742; Marshall, pp. 342-43.

CHAPTER VII

THE FEEDING OF THE FIVE THOUSAND

Mark 6:35-44

1. Recovering the Oral Tradition

Mark has shaped the introduction (vss. 30-34).[1] Vs. 37 is possibly a Markan polemic against the dis-disciples.[2] The reference to "green grass" may be a detail added by Mark to make the story accommodate the geographical setting in which Mark places it. The original setting appears to have been the wilderness. Vss. 35-36, 38-44 comprise the story.

> (35) And when it grew late, his disciples came to him and said, "This is a lonely place, and the hour is now late; (36) send them away to go into the country and villages around about and buy themselves something to eat. (38) And he said to them, "How many loaves have you? Go and see." And when they had found out they said, "Five and two fish." (39) Then he commanded them all to sit down by companies. (40) So they sat down in groups, by hundreds and by fifties. (41) And taking the five loaves and the two fish, he looked up to heaven and blessed and broke the loaves and gave them to the people; and he divided the two fish among them all. (42) And they all ate and were satisfied. (43) And they took up twelve baskets full of broken pieces and of the fish. (44) And those who ate the loaves were five thousand.

2. Interpretation of the Story

Throughout the critical period, scholars have variously regarded the pericope as a typology of Jesus

as the new Moses who gives manna in the wilderness, as
an anticipation of the messianic (or eschatological)
banquet, or as a tradition relating to the Lord's
Supper. Initially, then, we see that interpreters have
been interested in the meaning of the story as story.[3]

   A number of scholars have pointed to a typological
background in the Exodus narrative when the people of
Israel were fed by manna, or to the feeding of Elijah
by the ravens when the prophet was in the wilderness.
While some paper and ink has been devoted to establishing the connection with Elijah, the larger object
of interest has been a loose typology between the event
of manna in the wilderness and the event of the feeding
of the five thousand. The parallels emanating from
Ex. 16:4ff.[5] are: (1) Both events take place in the
wilderness; (2) Both involve bread; (3) In both a large
number of people are fed; (4) The same idea concludes
both accounts, "And the people ate and were satisfied."[6]

   Such parallels are inexact. ' Further, the gospel
narrative makes no overt allusion to the story of the
Exodus. As frequently presented, no account is taken
of the way in which the motif of manna in the wilderness might have been understood in popular religious
tradition at the time the story of the feeding of the
five thousand was first coming to expression. While
we may identify such a tradition, it is larger than
simply a typological relationship between the feeding
of Israel in the wilderness and the feeding of the
five thousand.[7]

   Two levels of interpretation may be detected in
the story: (1) The theme of the eschatological banquet which was (2) assimilated to the Lord's Supper.
It is difficult to know whether the assimilation was
made prior to Mark. In any case, vs. 41 is cast in
language which is more than casually reminiscent of
14:22. Further, when vs. 41 is removed and replaced
by a simpler vs., e.g. "and he took the bread and
the fish and gave it to them," the flow of the pericope is unchanged. In its present form, the vs. is not
essential.

   Of importance to the interpretation of the story
is its setting in the desert (or wilderness). For
the motif of the wilderness functions for this pericope
much as the sea functions in the story of the stilling
of the storm: the wilderness is a place hostile to

God and which threatens the life of the people of God. The wilderness must therefore be overcome.[8]

In the wandering traditions, the desert is a life-threatening place without food (Ex. 16:3) or water (Ex. 17:11, Num. 33:14). Divine guidance by pillar of cloud and fire is necessary for survival. The wilderness is the home of Azazael (Lev. 16:10).[9] While theophanies occur in the wilderness, they are the exception to the rule of desert living. Indeed, the wilderness is a place of punishment to which the children of Israel are sentenced for disobedience so that a whole generation may die.

Other traditions voice much the same feeling with regard to the desert. Sodom and Gomorrah, which were fertile regions, are turned into wastes (Gen. 19:24). The image of flourishing areas being turned into desert wastes is employed by the prophets as a sign of judgment (e.g. Jer. 4:23-28; Is. 34:11). Ezekiel uses the figure of the wilderness to describe "Egypt" (20:36). II Isaiah compares the destruction of Jerusalem by the Babylonians to a wilderness (51:3).

Further, in language with mythological overtones, the desert is described as a place which needs to be overcome and in which God must intervene in order for life to flourish. Ps. 68:6-7 implies that to live in the wilderness is to live beyond the normal care of God and thus requires God's providential action.[10] Is. 21:1 may compare the power of the desert to the power of the storming sea.[11] II Isaiah (34:8-15, 50:2) seems to imply that God must employ great power to defeat the desert in the same way that the sea must be turned back.[12] God delights not in chaos but in the orderly world (Is. 45:18).

Further, the wilderness is a habitation for demons. IV. Macc. 18:8 describes demons which wait in the wilderness to attack people and to lead them astray. A similar theme is voiced in Tobit 8:3. Is. 34:9-15 pictures the wilderness as the home of demonlike characters who have assumed animal form.

Therefore, it is not accidental that some traditions look forward to a time when the wilderness will be transformed by the power of God. It will no longer be life-threatening but will be life supporting. The creatures that live in it will be tamed and will give glory to God (Is. 35:9; Enoch 28:1). Of special

81

interest is the hope that God will feed the people in the wilderness (e.g. Is. 25:6; 65:13-14; Ps. 81:6).

The Qumran community deliberately settled itself in the desert for reasons that are not completely clear. But given their remarks on Is. 40:3 in IQS 8:12-16, they--and perhaps others of the time--regarded the wilderness as the place where the eschatological drama would take place. The period of salvation would begin in the desert.[13]

In the intertestamental literature, the theme of people being fed in the wilderness came to be amplified. Biblical scholars often speak rather loosely of a "messianic (or eschatological) banquet." Following the great Jewish tradition of meals as an occasion for celebration, the banquet accompanies the events of salvation. In fact, no paradigmatic description of such an event has been found. However, the motif of abundant feeding in the wilderness, which is pictured in the narrative of the feeding of the five thousand, was well known in popular Jewish literature of the first century.[14]

In an eschatological frame of reference, Is. 25: 6-8 looks forward to a remarkable meal to which God will invite all peoples. The context includes the defeat of death and a time of rejoicing in salvation. II Isaiah picks up the motif of being fed in the wilderness as the people journey from Babylon to their homeland (49:9ff.).

The metaphor of feasting is used to describe the nations coming together to share in the blessing of the covenant. Abundant food will be provided by the Lord for the restored nation (Ezek. 34:14ff). Zech. 9:17 sees the day of the Lord as a day of feasting. In several texts a day of feasting is preceded by the defeat of the enemies of God.

Many of these texts came to life during periods when basic needs for survival could not be taken for granted. Eating together at the banquet of God would mean more than a good meal in life-threatening circumstances. It would mean the triumph of God over a fundamental enemy.

This theme is intensified in apocalyptic literature. An oft-cited passage, IV Ezra 8:52-54, includes in the new era a description of it as an "age of plenty." Food will be abundant in the eschatological

reign. Enoch 62:14 mentions, briefly, eating with the
Messiah as a part of the state of the righteous.

II Baruch describes a remarkable meal in which
the sea will give up two fish and the earth will give
forth its fruit.

> And it shall come to pass when all is
> accomplished that was to come to pass in
> those parts, that the Messiah shall then
> begin to be revealed. And Behemoth shall
> be revealed from his place and Leviathan
> shall ascend from the sea, those two great
> monsters which I created on the fifth day
> of creation, and shall have kept until that
> time; and they shall be for food for all
> that are left. The earth shall also
> yield its fruit ten thousand and on each
> (?) vine there shall be a thousand branches,
> and each branch shall produce a thousand
> clusters, and each cluster produce a
> thousand grapes and each grape produce a
> cor of wine. And those who have hungered
> shall rejoice; moreover, also, they shall
> behold marvels every day. (29:3-7).

The author specifically refers to this food as manna--
the food of the wilderness (29:8) and the Sibylline
Oracle (7:149) repeats the same conviction.

Jean van Cangh finds, further, that II Baruch,
Enoch and IV Ezra all make reference to such a meal in
which great sea monsters are devoured. Behemoth and
Leviathan are interpreted as great symbols of chaos
who come up from the sea to be devoured (conquered)
by the congregation of the faithful at an eschatological banquet.[15]

The most detailed description of such a meal is
found in the literature of Qumran (IQSa 2:11-22; cf.
IQS 6:4-6). The first passage describes a communal
meal presided over by two messianic figures and gives
explicit instructions for serving bread and wine. At
the same time, the context is clear that these instructions are to be followed at every common meal of the
community. This leads G. Wainwright, following F.M.
Cross, to conclude that the communal meal at Qumran
is a kind of prototype or anticipation of the eschatological banquet.[16] The meal, taking place in the de-
sert--the very symbol of abandonment by God--is a time
of celebrating God's victory.

83

In all of these texts, the emphasis is not on the mechanics of the meal but on the abundance of the eschatological era. Life-threatening forces, as represented by the desert, are overcome by God and transformed into life-sustaining powers. This is an occasion for rejoicing such as is traditionally associated with meals, and particularly festival meals. Authors employ the traditional notion of satisfaction and fulfillment associated with meals to describe the feeling of the new era. In the larger context of apocalyptic, the food is part of the picture of fulfillment: the cycle of anxiety and tension caused by life-threats is broken.

The discipline of sociology of religion contributes to our understanding of this motif, and to apocalyptic in general, by pointing out that such themes usually come to expression during periods of unrest, when dreams have gone deferred. Alienated and oppressed groups are so bound and limited by their conditions that they can envision a change in circumstance only as a result of an extraordinary event. Their feelings and hopes are described in the metaphors and images of apocalyptic.[17]

Against this backdrop, the interpretation of the first level of the story is evident. The crowd is in a desert place, hungry, and without apparent resources. When fish and bread are brought to Jesus, he asks the crowd to sit down in groups of hundreds and fifties.[18] The loaves and fish are multiplied and distributed. The casual phrase toward the conclusion of the description of the scene, "and they were satisfied," may itself echo eschatologically. For those who eat the meal of the last age are expected to be filled.[19]

Now a significant difference between the feeding of the five thousand and the eschatological banquet is that those who were fed in the wilderness will hunger again. Thus the story could be taken as a sign of the dawning reign of God. But more than that, the story puts into picture-form the church's present experience. The desert, and what it stands for, is tamed.

Anne Wire correlates stories such as the feeding of the thousands with situations of scarcity and oppression and hunger.[20] The story of the feeding of the five thousand witnesses to the provision which the church finds. The least resources--like bread and fish--prove more than adequate in the presence of

Jesus.

When turning attention to the second layer of development, we note that while some interpreters have downplayed the relationship between the feeding of the thousands and the last supper, their efforts have been largely unsuccessful.[21] Two connections clearly support a eucharistic relationship.

The first is the unmistakable parallelism between the language of 6:41 and the language of 14:22.

> 6:41 And <u>taking</u> the five loaves and the
> two fish, he looked up to heaven
> and <u>blessed</u> and <u>broke</u> the loaves and
> <u>gave</u> them to the disciples . . . .

> 14:22 And as they were eating, he <u>took</u>
> bread and <u>blessed</u> and <u>broke</u> it and
> <u>gave</u> it to them . . . ·.

Such striking agreement would hardly be coincidental.

Secondly, the key words underlined in the two verses were quickly established as part of the technical eucharistic vocabulary of the early church.[22] To use these words would be to call to mind the Lord's Supper.

The similarity of language thus suggests that the feeding of the five thousand and the Lord's Supper allude to each other, but the inexactness of language suggests that the allusion is an <u>allusion</u> and not an attempt to equate the two meals. An early generation of Christians (though it is not clear how early) did celebrate a eucharist of fish and bread, and their texts may have been the feeding of the four and five thousands,[23] but the present narratives do not demand such an interpretation. The eucharistic narrative of Didache 9:4 makes use of the story of the feeding of the five thousand.[24]

Since the cultic language of the eucharist assumed fixed form at a very early stage of the tradition, and since the narratives of the feeding of the thousands could well have existed in an earlier form without the cultic language, it is likely that the cultic expression was transferred from the last supper to the feedings.[25]

In this way, the early church gave expression to its experience. The time of fulfillment described in the image of the eschatological banquet was enjoyed already in the Lord's Supper.[26] The feeling of the eschatological age was brought to life in the cultic drama. Thus Geoffrey Wainwright refers to this dimension of meaning in the Lord's Supper as the "antepast of heaven."[27]

Matthew's version of the story (14:13-21) has the disciples in a more important role than in either Mark or Luke. In addition to his other reshaping of the tale, this has led commentators to see the story as an illustration of discipleship.[28] When the disciples (i.e. the church) follow the instructions of Jesus, the multitude can be fed because the risen Lord is active in the church in the same way that Jesus is described as acting in the story. Because of similarities between the feeding and the Supper, Matthew may intend to say that the Lord is present in the Supper in the way that he was present at the feeding.[29]

Mark emphasizes the desert as a place of conflict between Jesus and Satan. We have, further, already suggested a reciprocal relationship between this story and the Lord's Supper. Because the power of God overcomes the power of Satan, even while the church is in the world, it can experience the victory associated with the messianic banquet through its participation in the Lord's Supper.[30] The disciples, however, are presented in Mark's characteristic way as lacking understanding. Their role is explained in Mark's doublet (8:1-21, esp. 14-21).

Luke's setting of the story (9:10-17) is specifically teaching about the reign of God (9:11). In his initial sermon, when Jesus was speaking about the nature of his ministry, Jesus specifically mentioned a feeding miracle performed by Elijah for the widow at Zarephath (4:25-26). From 10:13, we learn that Luke regarded the event of the feeding of the five thousand as an act of power. Luke had already prepared his readers to expect such powerful acts to be a part of the reign of God (e.g. 4:14, 36). The miracle is thus, for Luke, another example of what the reign of God is like and connection with the Lord's Supper is minimized.[31]

3. The Use of the Story in Preaching

The scene itself is rich with homiletical possibility: the wilderness. Whereas the crowd was in the wilderness of Judea, a traditional Jewish symbol for a place bereft of God, we often find ourselves in a modern wilderness which appears to be void of the symbols and presence of God. Yet, the story takes place precisely in the wilderness.

With whom do we identify in the story--the crowd or the disciples? While the two are not antithetical, neither do they function in the same way in the story.

If we identify with the crowd, we feel their hunger, their sense of scarcity as the sun sinks lower in the sky. They hunger for food, a basic need for survival. Few first world persons (especially few who would be in worship to hear a sermon on this text) have empty bellies. But many of us are afraid of the wilderness of this world and many--perhaps even the preacher--are hungry for purpose, fulfillment, direction and a sense of mission in life. Further, as we project the image onto the world situation, the scene is almost desperate. The sun seems sinking lower and lower, hidden behind a mountain range of nuclear missles and rising debts. We easily draw an analogy between the crowd in the darkening Judean desert and the situations of our congregation and our world.

The resources to resolve the crisis are pathetically small and ordinary. But when offered to Jesus they prove more than enough. Bread and fish we find around us everyday, but they feed hungry people. What are bread and fish to satisfy a congregation's hunger, a world's hunger? Can you offer them in a sermon?

As the story closes, we see people who once were hungry, now full, perhaps lounging in the sunset. A preacher might look for such a picture of fulfillment in the life of his or her congregation or community.

The disciples are concerned about the crowd. "This is a lonely place and the hour is now late." They recognize the need, but they assume that the enormity of the need is beyond their resources. "Send them away to go into the country and villages round about and buy themselves something to eat."

Ministers, lay leaders and congregations often want to be responsive to basic human need. But our resources often appear pathetic when contrasted with the size of the need.

As in the case of identifying with the crowd, the bread and fish, small and ordinary, when offered to Jesus prove abundant. What specifically are the bread and fish of our discipleship that we can place inside the sphere of values and influence shaped by Jesus?

A significant homiletical possibility is presented by the world hunger situation. People are literally starving to death. For them, hunger is no metaphor. The victims of the elements, of political and economic manipulation, they are powerless to leave the desert wastes, much less see the deserts transformed. In this scenario, we first world Christians are among the disciples who offer to Jesus our own resources for the feeding of the hungry. Our resources may appear insignificant in contrast to the world-wide structures of oppression which have a choke-hold on the hungry. Indeed, we may support those very structures by pursuing consumptive, self-centered lifestyles.

However, as we come into the sphere of the influence of Jesus, we discover that in order to be fulfilled, we do not need such self-gratification. Resources that we would have used to make our own lives more luxurious can be put at the disposal of the hungry. For example, a simple lifestyle can be our bread and fish. It can both make a practical difference in the feeding of hungry people and it can help change the structures of oppression. Simple living is not the whole answer, of course, but it may be bread and fish that I have in my hand right now. And when I offer it to Jesus, it may help break the circle of oppression.

Yet another homiletical possibility is to picture ways in which the Lord's Supper becomes a prefiguration of the eschatological banquet for the preacher's congregation. This may be difficult. For in many local churches the Lord's Supper is notoriously solemn, dull and even boring or morbid. Perhaps a sermon on this theme could help transform the congregation's sense of expectancy--or lack thereof--toward the Lord's Supper. The sermon itself could become an experience of "the joyful feast of the people of God" as the people partake via their imaginations.

[1]Pryke summarizes, p. 15. R. Fowler, Loaves and Fishes (Chico: Scholar's, 1981), pp. 69-81, argues that Mk. 6:30-44 is entirely a Markan composition, but his argument while impressive and painstaking, is not persuasive. See the literature in note 3.

[2]This is a difficult judgment. For while the motif appears in the parallels in Matt. 14:16-17/Lk. 9:13, it is heightened in Mk. The questioning of the disciples is missing in the doublets, Mk. 8:1-9/Matt. 15:32-39/Lk. 6:5-13.

[3]On the question of whether the story is a doublet of the feeding of the four thousand or a separate tradition, see the summary in G. Ziener, "Die Brotwunder im Markusevangelium," Bib 4 (1960), pp. 282-85; G. Friedrich, "Die Beiden Erzahlungen von der Speisung in Mark 6:31-44, 8:1-10," TZ 20 (1964), pp. 10-22 and J. Knockstadt, "Die Beiden Brotvermehrungen im Evangelium," NTS 10 (1964), pp. 309-35.

[4]II Kings 4:42ff. A comparison is sometimes drawn between 4:43 and Mk. 6:37.

[5]Fuller sees the Elijah story influencing the wording of the story of the feeding. Richardson sees a parallel between the story of the feeding and Elisha feeding 100 men with twenty loaves. That, however, is hardly "miraculous."

[6]Fuller, pp. 57-58; Nineham, p. 78; Richardson, p. 95.

[7]To be sure, motifs from the feeding of the people of Israel in the wilderness appear in the larger picture, e.g. the manna.

[8]Scholars have pointed to OT traditions which evaluate positively Israel's experience of wilderness. For example, Hos. 2:14ff., almost nostalgically recalls Israel's time in the wilderness as an ideal period in her relationship with God. But note that idealization is not of the wilderness per se, but of relationship. The basic study of the wilderness is still U. Mauser, Christ in the Wilderness, SBT (London: SCM, 1963). Cf. W.L. Reed, "Desert," IDB, vol. I, pp. 828-829; G. Kittel, "eramos," TDNT, Vol. II, p. 658; R. Funk, "The Wilderness," JBL 78 (1959), pp. 204-15; H.A. Kelly, "The Devil in the Desert," CBQ

26 (1964), pp. 190-220, and the updated material in S. Talmon, "Wilderness," IDB (Supplementary Volume), pp. 946-49.

[9] The desert is the home of fiery serpents (Nu. 21: 6), scorpions (Deut. 8:15), vultures (Zeph. 2:14), etc. Cf. Mauser, p. 37.

[10] Mauser, P. 42.

[11] Reed, p. 828.

[12] Mauser, p. 51.

[13] Kittel, p. 658; Mauser, p. 60.

[14] For literature in which the idea was kept alive in the religious memory, J. Behm, "deipnon," TDNT, Vol. II, p. 36 and Behm, "esthio," TDNT, Vol. II, p. 691; Boussett-Gressman, p. 285; J. Priest, "Messianic Banquet," IDB (Supplementary Volume), pp. 590-91; Strack-Billerbeck, Vol. IV, pp. 1154-165; G. Wainwright, Eucharist and Eschatology (New York: Oxford, 1971), pp. 19-29; J. Ross, "Meals," IDB, Vol. III, pp. 315-318.

[15] J.M. Van Cangh, "Le Theme des poissons dans le Recits evangeliques de la multiplication des pains," Revue Biblique 28 (1971), pp. 71-83. It is tempting to reach into mythology for a background. In the Akkadian Adapa myth, we learn that Adapa is the one who prepares bread and does the fishing. Thus at the primeval level, bread and fish are conjoined. They are necessary for life and are projected into the heavenly chamber since Adapa was created as a model to be followed by human beings. Even more interesting is the motif of the quest for immortality on which Adapa sets but which he is unable to complete. He longs to eat the bread of life, but is not able, even when it is set before him. His creator, Ea, has forbidden it. At one point, when he speaks of earth he speaks of going down to where the fish are, as if the fish reside in and are subservient to the demon of chaos. (Pritchard, Vol. I, pp.76-79). It is extremely tenuous to attempt to trace this theme through the OT. To be sure, there is considerable mention of bread as a symbol for the food which is necessary for life and is therefore longed for (Ps. 37:25; 70:20-28; 104:15; 105:40; 132:15; Prov. 25:21; 28:21; Isl 51:14). I find, however, no connection between bread and fish.

Fish are sometimes represented in art as dwelling in the sea with the powers of chaos (W. McCullough, "Fish," IDB, Vol. 2, p. 273). E.R. Goodenough, _Jewish Symbols in the Greco-Roman Period_ (New York: Pantheon, 1965), vol. XII, pp. 94ff., thinks a meal of fish bespoke immortality and that fish were expected to be eaten in the messianic age (Vol. I, p. 50). However, the evidence cited is all much later than the NT.

[16]Wainwright, p. 25; cf. L. Bodia, _The Dead Sea People's Sacred Meal and Jesus' Last Supper_ (Washington, D.C.: University Press of America, 1979); E. Stauffer, "Zum Apokalyptischen Festmahl in Mc 6:34ff." ZNW 46 (1955), pp. 264-66; G. Vermes, _The Dead Sea Scrolls: Qumran in Perspective_ (Philadelphia: Fortress, 1981), pp. 94, 126, 182 and the bibliography p. 193; I.H. Marshall, _Last Supper and Lord's Supper_ (Grand Rapids: Eerdmans, 1980), pp. 13-29, esp. 18-20 and 23-26.

[17]M. Weber, _The Sociology of Religion,_ tr. E. Fischoff (Boston: Beacon, 1963), pp. 80, 106-07, followed by P. Hanson, _The Dawn of Apocalyptic_, rev. ed. (Philadelphia: Fortress, 1979), pp. 211-217.

[18]In so doing, **the story may make use** of a gesture which would have **been popularly associated with** the eschatological age; see IQSa 2:1-22 and Vermes, _The Dead Sea Scrolls in English_, pp. 16-17.

[19]Citations in G. Delling, "_plaras_," TDNT, Vol. VI, pp. 288, 302.

[20]Wire, pp. 96-99.

[21]E.g. G.H. Boobyer, "The Eucharistic Interpretation of the Miracle of the Loaves in St. Mark's Gospel," JTS (1952), pp. 161. Boobyer's strongest argument is that the language of vs. 41 is paralleled in Acts 27:35 and that similar words were used at any Jewish meal. He does not take account of the developed eucharistic tradition. Cf. Schwiezer, _Mark_, p. 139 and note 22.

[22]J. Jeremias, _The Eucharistic Words of Jesus_, tr. N. Perrin (Philadelphia: Fortress, 1966), pp. 174-76; Marshall, pp. 40-51; Wainwright, pp. 35-36 and the commentaries, _ad loc_.

[23]Richardson, p. 96, and more recently, R. Heirs,

and C. Kennedy, "Bread and Fish Eucharist in the Gospels and Early Christian Art," _Perspectives in Religious Studies_ 3 (1976), pp. 20-47.

[24]L. Cerfaux, "La Multiplication des pains dans la liturgie de la Didache," _Biblica_ 40 (1959), pp. 943-58.

[25]This is carefully developed in Achtemeier, "Origin and Function," to whom I am much indebted.

[26]Other scholars see the central significance of the stories of the feedings in their numerology. Twelve, for instance is said to stand for Jews while seven represents Gentiles. G.H. Boobyer, "Miracles of the Loaves and St. Mark's Gospel," SJT (1953), pp. 77-87; A. Farrar, "Loaves and Thousands," JTS 4 (1953), pp. 1-14; A. Shaw, "Marcan Feeding Narratives," _Church Quarterly Review_ 162 (1961), pp. 268-78; B.F. Thiering, "Breaking of Bread and Harvest in St. Mark's Gospel," NT 12 (1970_, pp. 1-12.

[27]Wainwright, p. 18.

[28]Held, pp. 182-83.

[29]Gundry, pp. 293-95; Schweizer, _Matthew_, p. 319.

[30]See above, pp. 82-83.

[31]Luke's eucharistic passage has the word "give thanks" in place of the present word "blessed." Fitzmyer, p. 764; Marshall, pp. 361-62; Cf. Conzelmann, pp. 51-52.

CHAPTER VIII

THE HEALING OF BLIND BARTIMAEUS

Mark 10:46-52

1. Recovering the Oral Tradition

Mark has created the seam in 10:46ab as well as the conclusion in 52c, "And followed him on the way."[1] The name Bartimaeus is likely pre-Markan but perhaps not a part of the oldest tradition.[2] The strata would read much like this.

> Bartimaeus, a blind beggar, was sitting by the side of the road. (47) And when he heard that it was Jesus of Nazareth passing by, he cried out, "Jesus, (?Son of David?), have mercy on me." (48) And many rebuked him, telling him to be silent; but he cried out all the more. (49) And Jesus stopped and said, "Call him." And they called the blind man, saying to him, "Take heart, rise, he is calling you." (50) And throwing off his mantle, he sprang up and came to Jesus. (51) And Jesus said to him, "What do you want me to do for you?" And the blind man said to him, "Master, let me receive my sight." (52) And Jesus said to him, "Go your way, your faith has made you well." And immediately, he received his sight."

2. Interpretation of the Story

Particularly at the third level of tradition, and particularly in its present context in the gospel of Mark, much interpretative attention has been given to the symbolic use of the story. While precise evaluations of the use of the story vary, the general thrust is that it symbolizes what needs to happen to the

disciples or to the crowd or to the prospective believer: their eyes need to be opened, i.e., they need
to perceive rightly the nature of Jesus' ministry as
well as the nature of discipleship.[3]

The motif of blindness and coming to sight is a
key to understanding the story. The motif has a rich
and important background. Our interpretation will be
helped if we recall the associations first century
persons would have had when they heard that the story
was about a blind beggar.

Throughout the Mediterranean world, blindness was
a prevalent and prominent disease. Resulting from a
variety of causes, it manifested itself in very pro-
nounced affliction of the eyes in such ways as inflammation, swelling, running pus, the covering of the
eyes with a glaze. The glaring sun, the wind (carrying
dust) and flies irritated the condition of the eyes
and frequently accentuated their already gruesome ap-
pearance.[4] To call to mind a blind person is likely
to call to mind such a misshapen face.

The OT does not contain an extended description
of the life of the blind. But it is noteworthy that
at least by the time of the formation of the Pentateuch
the social consequences of blindness were considered
serious enough that the blind were protected by legis-
lation. For example, no stumbling block is to be
placed in front of the blind (Lev. 19:14) and anyone
who leads a blind person astray is declared cursed
(Deut. 27:8). Such protection was continued in the
later interpretation of the Old Testament.[5] Job takes
pride in having been obedient to the concern for the
poor and blind (29:12-17).

Closer to the time of the NT, the book of Tobit
tells the story of a righteous man (Tobit) who becomes
blind when the dung of sparrows settles in his eyes
(2:10). He must be led by the hand wherever he goes
and his life gradually degenerates until he cries
out. Perhaps he voices the feeling of the time regarding blindness. "What cheer have I any more, who
am a man impotent in the eyes, and I behold not the
light of heaven but lie in darkness like the dead
which no more see the light; while I live I am among
the dead" (5:17). To be blind is to lie in darkness
like the dead.[6]

Blindness is one of the "blemishes" which renders
an animal unfit for sacrifice to the Lord (Deut. 15:21,

Lev. 22:22). Blindness can be administered by God as a curse for refusing to hear the words of the Lord and for refusing to keep the commandments (Deut. 28:28). In the Qumran community, the blind are forbidden to fight in the eschatological battle (IQM 7:4) and are not permitted to partake in the community/eschatological meal (IQSa 2:3-6). Thus in many quarters the blind (with others who are considered "blemished") are disqualified from approaching too near the symbols of holiness.

While a few blind persons achieved notable positions in the ancient world, the vast majority lived in severe poverty and made their living as beggars.[7] While the righteous were expected to give to the poor, begging was by no means a desirable way of life (e.g. I Sam. 2:36) and is invoked as a curse on the wicked (Ps. 109:10). The Septuagint of II Sam. 5:8 forbids beggars from complete access to the temple.[8] A tractate later than the NT but which may record an attitude alive in the first half of the first century, forbids those who have medical infirmities that would render them unclean from entering the temple further than the court of the Gentiles.[9]

Sirach 40:28-29 may describe the feeling which prevailed toward beggars (and which beggars may have had toward themselves).

> My son, live not a beggar's life;
> Better is one dead than importunate.
> A man that looketh to a stranger's table--
> His life is not to be reckoned as a
> life:
> A pollution of his soul are the dainties
> presented,
> And to an understanding man inward
> torture.
> In the mouth of an insatiable (man) begging
> is sweet,
> But inwardly it burneth as fire.
> (40:28-30).

While Jewish law attempted to protect the welfare of the blind, to be blind was to have one's freedom severely restricted, to suffer from the painful infirmity and to be regarded religiously as "blemished," i.e. almost outside the realm of divine usefulness. Thus, in addition to calling to mind the physical characteristics of the blind, the mention of a blind man sitting alongside the road begging would bring

to consciousness the feelings associated with his
place in ancient life.

Not surprisingly, in contexts which voice the
longing for the renewal of the nation's situation or
which look forward to the eschatological renewal of
the cosmos, some of the classical prophets and others
anticipate God opening the eyes of the blind.

> Is it not yet a very little while
>   until Lebanon shall be turned into a
>   fruitful field,
> and the fruitful field shall be regarded
>   as a forest?
> In that day the deaf shall hear the words
>   of a book,
> and out of their gloom and darkness
>   the eyes of the blind shall see.
>   (Is. 29:17-18)

> Then the eyes of the blind shall be
>   opened,
>   and the ears of the deaf unstopped;
> Then shall the lame man leap like a hart
>   and the tongue of the dumb sing for joy.
> For waters shall break forth in the
>   wilderness,
>   and streams in the desert;
> the burning sand shall become a pool,
>   and the thirsty ground springs of water;
> the haunt of jackals shall become a swamp,
>   the grass shall become reeds and rushes.
>   (Is. 35:5-7).

Admittedly it is sometimes difficult to determine whether a reference is to a physical healing or to the
recovery of spiritual perception.

Without specifically mentioning the opening of
the eyes of the blind, II Baruch (speaking for many of
the apocalyptic writers) depicts the messianic age.

> And it shall come to pass. when He has brought
>   low everything that is in the world,
> And has sat down in peace for the age on
>   the throne of his kingdom,
> That joy shall then be revealed
> And rest shall appear.

> And healing shall descend in dew,
> And disease shall withdraw,

And anxiety and anguish and lamentation
    shall pass from among men,
And gladness proceed through the whole earth.

And no one shall die untimely,
Nor shall any adversity suddenly befall.
                    (73:1-3).

Later Judaism, too, looked forward to the healing of
the blind as part of the eschatological age.[10] The
image of the recovery of sight of the blind under the
influence of the eschatological age is thus a familiar
one.

    Against this background, we also find a rich tra-
dition in which the motif of blindness is used in a
figurative sense. Associations with physical blindness
are transferred to metaphors and images in order to
describe the perceptual state of individuals and com-
munities. Persons can be described as intellectually,
morally and spiritually blind.

    A frequent use is in figures of speech for the
purposes of comparison. The Lord will cause those who
violate the covenant to "grope at noonday as the blind
grope in darkness" (Deut. 28:29). II Isaiah uses
much the same comparison describing the lot of the
exiles (59:10). Zephaniah, too, quotes the Lord as
bringing such distress on sinners that they will "walk
like the blind" (1:17). Matthew makes use of the
popular figure of the "blind leading the blind" (Matt.
15:14).[11]

    Of the classical prophets, II Isaiah employs the
transferred sense most extensively, often in reference
to those who cannot perceive the redemptive activity
of God.[12]

        Bring forth the people who are blind,
            yet have eyes,
        who are deaf,
            yet have ears.   (43:8).

The exiles look for light but instead see only darkness, groping like the blind; "among those in full vi-
gor, we are like the dead" (59:9-10). The watchers are
themselves blind (56:10). A part of the mission of
the servant and ultimately of the servant community is
described in a similar metaphor.

> I am the Lord, I have called you in
> > righteousness,
> I have taken you by the hand and kept you;
> I have given you as a covenant to the
> > people,
> > a light to the nations
> > to open the eyes that are blind,
> to bring out the prisoners from the dun-
> > geon,
> > from the prison those who sit in
> > darkness. (42:6-7).[13]

Opening the eyes of the blind would become a part of
the Septuagint text of Is. 61:1.

The transferred sense can also be found in other
literature in the neighborhood of the time of the NT.
The Qumran community used the image of blindness (IQS
4:11) in a catalogue of vices which begins with greed
and ends with the notation that persons with such
qualities "walk in the ways of darkness." In the Da-
mascus Rule, blindness is used to picture Israel's
quest for God. Israel was like a blind person groping
for direction (CD 1:6).

Of other apocalyptic literature, the Testaments
of the Twelve Patriaches makes frequent use of the
metaphor of blindness. The last of the seven spirits
of deceit (the corruption of sexual power) will lead
young people like the blind falling into a pit (T. Re.
2:9). Simeon's mind was blinded by the spirit of deceit so that he no longer looked upon Joseph as his
brother (T. Si. 2:7). Likewise, the impulse of youth
blinded Judah to the wickedness of the Canaanites (T.
Ju. 11:1); in particular, love of money and fornication
will "blind the inclination of the soul" (18:3,6).
The variant readings of T. Dan 2:2 functionally equate
blindness and anger; the angry person is unable to perceive "the face of any man with truth."

The story of Ahikar compares two types of blindness.

> O my son, the blindness of the heart
> is more grievous than the blindness of
> the eyes, for the blindness of the eye
> may be guided little by little, but
> the blindness of the heart is not guided,
> and it leaves the straight path and
> goes in a crooked way. (2:48).[14]

The Midrashim and Targums, though late, use the figure of blindness to refer to the lack of receptivity to the Torah and to other religious instruction.[15]

Thus we see that the literature of Judaism had a tradition of using the known plight of the physically blind in order to speak about imperceptivity. Because the literal and metaphorical meanings often intermingle and are difficult to separate, one must be careful not to say that that the meaning of a verse or pericope has been exhausted by too quickly referring to one or the other.

On one level, the story of the opening of the eyes of blind Bartimaeus seems to be nothing more than an account of a healing. But on another level, it may be a story which uses the figure of the opening of the eyes of blind Bartimaeus to dramatize the experience of the church. To paraphrase the popular hymn, "We once were blind, but now we see." The story of the healing becomes a metaphor to describe the experience of coming to live in the sphere of the authority of Jesus.

This possibility is strengthened when we realize that the OT, the literature of intertestamental and post-Biblical Judaism, often speak of the redemptive acts of God or the age of salvation as being <u>seen</u>.[16] Once again we find the intermingling of the literal and the metaphorical. Theophanies habitually include a visual component[17] as do the visions of the prophets.[18] Moses tells the children of Israel, mashed between the Egyptians and the Red Sea, to "stand firm and see the salvation of God" (Ex. 14:13). Through the pen of the Psalmist, the Lord promises to "show salvation" to those who cleave to God in love (91:16) while the 119th Psalmist regrets that his or her eyes fail while watching for salvation (119:123). II Isaiah frequently connects the motif of seeing with spiritual perception (e.g. 52:10; 59:11, 16).[19]

The Community Rule of Qumran confirms,

> For my light has sprung
>   from the source of His knowledge;
> My eyes have beheld his marvellous deeds,
>   and the light of my heart, the mystery
>   to come. (IQS 11:2-3).

And in a hymn, following a break in the text, the singer asks,

99

(How) shall I look,
   unless Thou open my eyes?
Or hear
   (unless Thou unstop my ears)?
My heart is astounded
for to the uncircumcised ear
   a word has been disclosed,
and a heart (of stone
   has understood the right precepts).
               (IQH 18:5).

Likewise, Gad is made to testify, "These things I learnt at last, after I had repented concerning Joseph. For true repentance after a godly sort (destroyeth ignorance and) driveth away the darkness and enlighteneth the eyes, and giveth knowledge to the soul and leadeth the mind to salvation" (T. Gad 5:6-7).

We see, then, that preachers and teachers of the early church had available to them a recognized tradition which used blindness and sight in metaphorical ways. That NT writers were aware of this tradition is apparent from passages like II Cor. 4:4, Ro. 2:19, Matt. 15:14/Lk. 6:39, Matt. 23:16-24, II Pet. 1:9 and John 9. In particular we see that residents of the first century would be able to understand the story of a blind man coming to sight as a pictorial way of describing spiritual activity.

The church has come to see that in Jesus, God is engaged in redemption. This discovery is so potent and powerful that it can be described in the graphic image of the blind man being healed. Through participation in the story, by identifying with the blind man, listeners and readers can accompany him on his transformational journey from the side of the road to having his sight restored.

In connection with the story of the woman with the issue of blood, we found that faith is the means by which one is transferred from the old, blind realm to the new. The repetition of the phrase, "Your faith has made you well," suggests that the phrase was stylized in the tradition. The pericope, then, is a picture of what it is like to find oneself **transferred** from one realm of values and experience to another.

Commentators have noticed this theme. Dibelius, for instance, writes, "Every blind beggar may experience the same thing as Bartimaeus."[20] Nineham thinks that when the story was spoken in the early church, "it was in order to hold him up as a model to believers and would-be believers."[21] Schrage cautions against limiting the story to either a physical healing or to being a "mere symbol."[22] Richardson, taking the spiritual route of interpretation sees all people sitting like beggars until Jesus appears.[23] Hauck follows that the blind man is a counterpart of all the blind.[24] Amos Wilder penetrates with his usual skill.

> For the first believers, it was a condensation of their faith. It would be an error to limit its signification to the physical healing. When the blind beggar Bartimaeus pressed his cry . . . he spoke for all who looked for the new age and its redemption. The special case of blindness is here secondary to the generic situation that human life is set about with what we call fatality and the inexorable . . . . The healing and others like it had this more general significance already in the activity of Jesus himself.[25]

The primitive community may have taken up the story precisely because it symbolized human experience. Not only does it tell of the recovery of physical sight but it describes how blindness of the self to divine activity in the world is removed. Not only that, but the same recovery of sight is available to the hearers of the story: by faith. As we trust the realm shaped by the values and presence of Jesus, we find our eyes opened.

Matthew not only adds another blind person to the story as he retells it, but he tells it twice (9:27-31; 20:29-34). Matthew edits the stories so that the first interprets the second. By placing the conversation at the heart of the pericopae, Matthew uses the stories to illustrate the larger theme of faith.[26] In the first story, the healed ones become proclaimers (9:31) while in the second they are explicitly identified as becoming disciples (20:34).[27] The stories, therefore, serve as both metaphors of healing and as paradigms for the healed. The first also provides an example to complete the list in 11:5. As we have frequently commented, these are also the ministry which is given to the disciples and the church.

Mark uses the story as a model of what must happen to the disciples. Hitherto they have been blind to

nature and purpose of the ministry of Jesus, particularly to the necessity of his suffering and death and
to the mode of discipleship which is shaped by suffering. The pericope functions for Mark as a model of
discipleship.[28] The eyes of the disciples must be
opened.

Luke (18:35-43) reduces interest in the blind
person by leaving out personal references and by situa-
ting Jesus at the center of the narrative.[29] Luke
places the story as part of the climax of Jesus' ministry to the poor and outcast. Further, Luke reports ex-
ceptional praise both from the healed man and from the
onlookers, thereby inviting his readers to do the same
and to affirm the ministry to the poor and outcast.[30]

3. The Use of the Story in Preaching

The metaphorical possibility of the motif of the
opening of the eyes of the blind has long been recognized. So great is the transition from one realm of
experience to another that the hymn affirms, "I once
was blind, but now I see."

As we prepare to preach from the story at the level of oral tradition, a natural point of identification is with the blind beggar. As the story opens,
we sit with him alongside the road. What would it
feel like to be there? Physical sensations? Emotions?

Blindness creates a world of limited perception.
In the town in which I grew up, a girl born blind mar-
ried, raised children, established her own telephone
answering service and travelled extensively with her
family. After her retirement, an advanced surgical
procedure allowed her to see. Even though she had
constructed "images" of people, places and things, her
frame of reference had been distorted.

We, too, are afflicted with the inability to
perceive. Sometimes my need to push for the success
of a program in the church blinds me from seeing my
parishoner's erratic, irresponsible, even irrational
and destructive behaviour as a cry for help. Sometimes
I cannot see my wife's actions as expressing real and
genuine concern for me and for our relationship. My
soft, relatively luxurious middle class lifestyle
obscures my perception of God's liberating activity in
behalf of the poor and oppressed. My almost unconscious identification with the success syndrome of our

102

culture often fogs my sensitivity to that power which is revealed in the cross.

Indeed, so debilitating does our darkness become that in our own words, we sometimes join the beggar's cry. "Have mercy on us!" In my own life, how do I sense and express that longing to be healed? How do I hear it in the life of my congregation? In our culture? In our world?

Jesus of Nazareth does not physically pass by, of course, but when I come into contact with a reality shaped by his values and presence, I can see. Perhaps that reality is a person, a community, a writing, a media event. In preaching, I hope to illustrate the recovery of sight as vividly as does the Biblical story, and as vividly as I have described blindness.

The story ends on an unspoken, unintended, ironic note. The beggar has received his sight, but now he is out of a job. Sometimes coming to sight changes the structures of life in just that way.

NOTES

[1] Summaries of research in R. Patten, pp. 112-114, 257; P. Patten, p. 136; Pryke, p. 19; Cf. nn. 2-3.

[2] Bultmann, HST, p. 213; Dibelius, pp. 52-53; Hauck, p. 131; Nineham, p. 285; Taylor, p. 447.

[3] V. Robbins gives a history of research, "The Healing of Blind Bartimaeus," JBL 92 (1973), pp. 224-225.

[4] R.K. Harrison, "Blindness," IDB, Vol. I, p. 448.

[5] W. Schrage, "tuphlos," TDNT, Vol. VIII, pp. 282-83.

[6] Fish gall enables Tobit to see again (11:12). Other similar instances of the healing of blindness are recorded in ancient literature, but the main hope for the blind in Judaism is in God.

[7] Schrage, p. 275; W. Michaelis, "orao," TDNT, Vol. V, p. 347.

[8]J. Jeremias, _Jerusalem in the Time of Jesus_, tr. F. and C. Cave (London: SCM, 1969), p. 117.

[9]_Ibid._

[10]Schrage, pp. 284-85. However, his exx. are all from literature later than the NT.

[11]For comparisons using the figure of the blind in the non-Hebrew world of antiquity, Schrage, pp. 275-76.

[12]_Ibid._, p. 281.

[13]The servant himself seems to be blind (42:19) but, paradoxically removes the blindness of others. On the difficulty of the motif, compare J. Muilenburg, "Isaiah, Chapters 40-66," IB, Vol. V, p. 476 and C. Westermann, _Isaiah 40-66_, tr. D. Stalker (Philadelphia: Westminster, 1969), p. 110.

[14]The quote is from the Arabic manuscript. The Syriac manuscript gives the same idea.

[15]Schrage, pp. 284-85.

[16]E.S. Johnson, "Mark 10:46-52: Blind Bartimaeus," CBQ 40 (1978), p. 201, following Michaelis, pp. 339-40, 346f.

[17]Michaelis, p. 331.

[18]_Ibid._, pp. 329-30.

[19]For God to "see" a situation is for God to understand it.

[20]Dibelius, p. 118.

[21]Nineham, p. 283.

[22]Schrage, p. 289.

[23]Richardson, p. 89.

[24]Hauck, p. 130.

[25]A. Wilder, _Early Christian Rhetoric: The Language of the Gospel_ (Cambridge: Harvard, 1971), p. 63.

[26]Held, p. 178; Schweizer, _Matthew_, p. 230.

[27]Schweizer, _Matthew_, p. 399. The verb "to follow" is here used as a technical expression for discipleship.

[28]Schweizer, _Mark_, p. 224; E. Johnson, pp. 198-202. For an analysis of the story as a call narrative, P. Achtemeier, "And He Followed Him: Miracle and Discipleship in Mark 10:46-52," _Semeia_ 11 (1978), pp. 115-145.

[29]Achtemeier, "The Lukan Perspective," p. 155; Held, p. 222.

[30]Marshall, p. 693.

CHAPTER IX

THE HERMENEUTICAL MOVEMENT

Three Sermons

Each of the following sermons was preached at
First Christian Church (Disciples of Christ), Grand
Island, Nebraska. Preaching is a community event. It
rises from the interaction of Biblical and theological
traditions with the life of a community located in a
specific time and place. Preaching both reflects the
life (and imagery) of the community and it seeks to ad-
dress that life. Historically conditioned, sermons belong to the people, place and time in which they are
preached.

I remove these three sermons from their historical
context and translate them from their native oral form
into the relatively unnatural medium of print in order
to illustrate the hermeneutical movement. I seek only
to show how one pastor moved from text to sermon.

The population of Grand Island is roughly 40,000
and its economy is agriculturally based, primarily tied
to corn, wheat, soybeans, sorghum and beef. A sub-
stantial Hispanic population is the only large nonwhite
ethnic group, though the Asian-American population is
growing. Solidly middle class, it is the major medical
and shopping center in central Nebraska. Many people
can still trace their ancestral roots back to Central
Europe. The community takes pride in being an "All
American City."

The congregation numbers 350, with approximately
equal numbers of senior members, middle aged, young
adults, youth and children. With more blue than white
collar workers, the congregation tends to be conservative in politics, finance and theology. Members frequently say that in preaching they like to "hear the
Bible." Technical theological jargon must be avoided.
In the best sense, they are "down home" folks.

The sermons are addressed to the church community
and are based on the pertinent exegetical remarks in
the preceding chapters. Because they are time-bound, I
have retained local references. Exegeses which lifted
up other themes or which took place in other communi-
ties would necessarily result in different sermons.

1.   The Still in the Storm (Mark 4:35-41)

The lightning forked across the sky
   jagged and raw
      casting into silhouette
      the rounded hills.
The white froth of the boiling waves
   ghostly in the flickering light
      grabs the boat with its pale hands
     and pulls it do_{w_n}
             into the black belly
             of the sea.
Their eyes squinting against the wind,
   their faces ashen as the weathered wood of the boat,
     their clothes wet
       heavy and chafing against the skin,
     their hearts sinking
       with every wave driving over the side,
         pulling the boat lower
           into
             the
               black
                 belly
                  of
                   the
                    sea.

What can a fragile person do
   when the water is coming over the side
     and it feels like
       the boat is about to go down?

Even in Nebraska
   we know the power of water uncontrolled.
     The Platte, a mile wide and an inch deep now,
       in a few churning moments
         can be twelve miles wide and twelve feet
           deep.
     In the flood of 1967,
       a woman stood at the top of the basement steps
         watching the water bubble up
           between the tiles in the floor

                    like little springs
                         filling the basement up,
                      and all she could do
                             was sit on the top step
                             and cry.

Sometimes I think life is like the water,
    quiet and peaceful and calm,
       alive with sparkling light,
          and then in a few churning moments
             the cloud comes
                 the lightning forks jagged and raw
                   and we feel like we're on a boat,
                      tossed and turned
                         "every which way but loose,"
                   and sometimes it feels like
                      life is out of control
                         like we're going under.
                             Glug.
                             Glug.
                             Glug.

An olive branch is extended to China
    and the Russians start rattling their missiles
       like **dice in a canister**
The people's hero returns to Iran,
    and his first statement,
       delivered as casually
          as if he were asking directions
             to the men's room
                is that Westerners
                   should leave
                      or their hands
                         may leave the country
                             separated from their arms.
We saw on TV
    a new development in national defense,
       a kind of a microwave oven floating in space
          that can shoot a beam of energy
             at a flying missile
                and disintegrate the missile
                   like a child blowing a dandelion.
    I wonder if it can distinguish
             between missiles
                and skyscrapers
                   and farmer's silos
                      and church spires.
    A girl says, "I don't like Mondays."
       "They bore me."
             And so she takes a rifle off the shelf
                and points it out her bedroom window

and kills two people.
What kind of boat are we riding in
that girls think guns are oars?
There is a little girl, almost three
with a bouncy pony tail
and a red checked long dress
trying to ride her little boat
to her Sunday School class
but when her parents turn to leave
she cries enough
to make the Wood River flood.
It might even be easier
to be on a boat
on a storm-tossed sea
than to be a youth
eye-ball to eye-ball
with an angry parent.
A parent who gave us life,
who loved us when we weren't worth loving,
who trusted us when we weren't worth trusting,
gets old
wrinkled in mind as well as in skin,
and what do we do?
What is right for them?
What is right for us?
The phone rings in the middle of the night
and we stand there on the cold floor
in bare feet
heart colder than the floor,
because he's gone
or she's gone
and someday we'll be gone.

Sometimes we feel like the disciples
pale in the ashen light
clothes heavy with water
the lightning jagged and raw
forking across the sky,
"Master, save us!
We're about to go under!"

Perhaps it is comforting
to know that Jesus is in the boat with us,
but . . . he is asleep.
Asleep?
How can he be asleep
with the storm of life thrashing us?
How can he sleep through
missiles rattling like dice
rifle shots on Monday

```
                    little girls crying
                       death stalking the earth?
        So we take him by the shoulders
           and shake him awake.

        And the wind dropped,
           and there was a great calm
              not for a lifetime
                 but for a moment.
        The sea would storm again
           and the storm would follow them
              gathering its thunderheads among the
                       the Pharisees
                       the Sadduccees
                       the Priests
                       the Scribes
                  .    and finally
                       in the heart of the people
                          until the sky turned dark
                             when the nails
                                were driven in his hands

        That day on the sea was only a moment of calm
           but it was a moment,
              and it was enough
                 to send them
                    onto the sea again
                       and again
                          and again.

     Those moments of calm
        as if someone has rebuked the storm.
           Someone has been on our backs,
              or maybe we've made a gigantic mistake
                 in running the church
                    and we get to feeling
                       "What's the use?"
                          and all there is to do
                             is pray
                             and go to bed
                             and rub each other's backs
                                as the wind strokes the
                                prairie
                                   and for a moment
                                      all is calm.
        Only one person shows up for a meeting,
           and you get the message that nobody cares
              and the ship you are piloting
                 is really s i
                               n k i
                                    ng,
```

then you and that someone else
share a few moments
and something inside
begins to tingle
and take water
and grow.
Our ad for the Christmas Eve Service
tried to describe the way
some of us were feeling,
"Aching feet?
Jangled nerves?
Tired eyes?
Hands tense as THE deadline comes?"
But when the time came
and the candles were burning,
we really didn't wonder as we wandered,
because for an hour
we felt the peace
that passeth all understanding.
At the time of death,
sometimes the family will laugh,
laugh until they weep,
as they remember something
from that life
that made him or her so special.

What does Jesus have to do with moments like these?
As far as I can tell,
in the New Testament
he is the one who speaks the word of rebuke
and brings the calm out of the storm
if only for the moment
that is a moment.

It was a big, white, rambling three-story
Victorian house,
with a porch on three sides
an attic big enough for a gymnasium
servants quarters on the back
and an English sheepdog named Bumbee.
But in the wake of divorce
the books wouldn't balance
and roomers moved in.
In the basement the "rainbow man,"
wire rim glasses
Mississippi accent
who made rainbows--
of wood--for a living.
Into the servants quarters
a student,
lean

                    tall
                    bearded
                    hungry-looking,
          and the curator
                    quiet and bearded
                    every fold of his clothes in place
                    and every hair in line,
                    his voice as gentle as spring moss
     The mother going back to school
          trying to pick up the pieces
               of her broken life
                    before they got lost
                         never to be found.
     The daughter tall and willowy
          pretty as the first daffodil
               breaking through
                    the last crust of snow.

With the sunlight splashing through the morning
windows,
     we all went to our separate days,
          returning in the evening,
               sitting around the table
                    soft with lamplight
                         eating
                         sharing the pain of a bad experience
                         laughing at some buffoonery
                         singing
                         and going into the night
                              with a lift in the heart.
     The sea was quiet,
          sparkling,
               the kind poets write about.

I never knew quite what caused
     the thunder to crash
          the lightning to fork
               but over our happy little boat
                    waves boiled up
                         from unexplained,
                              unseen
                                   sources.
     It was like somebody carved a hole in my chest,
          and my feelings just dribbled out.
     Coming and going,
          we didn't cross paths,
               and I remember standing behind our door
                    waiting for someone to pass
                         before I padded quietly and quickly
                              down the stairs.
Human feelings are delicate,

```
            and sometimes
          we treat each other
            with all the tenderness
              of jackhammers.

  We moved our cooking downstairs
      into the dank whitewashed basement
        with wooden slats across the floor.
    The curator had just finished an exhibit
        on veneral disease
          and he had yards and yards
              of blue fabric
                  on which the pictures
                    had been pinned.
        He hung it on the wall
          and called it "V.D. Blue,"
            and sometimes we called our songs,
              "Singing the VD Blues."
    And I remember how it happened
        that after a short-circuit upstairs
          we had our hands joined in prayer
            and one thin voice
                began to sing all by itself,
                  "Praise God from whom
                      all blessings flow,"
    and I remember how peaceful it felt,
      at least for that moment.

Yes, the lake would again froth and boil
    and the lightning would fork,
        and that's life.
But the moment of calm was real.

Maybe it is a miracle
    that Jesus gives us any peace at all,
        and maybe that peace is reason enough
            to turn
              and look
                and ask,
                    "What manner of man is this?"
```

2. Bread in the Wilderness (Mark 6:35-44)

God must eat Wheaties by the bushel, for God
never seems to tire of revealing what God's reign—or
God's Kingdom—is like. While some of the pictures of
God's reign are as dignified as a family portrait
hanging over the fireplace, others are strange and almost bizarre.

For instance, Malachi asks, "Who can endure the day of his coming and who can stand when he appears? For he is like a refiner's fire . . . and he will purify the sons of Levi and refine them like silver and gold" (3:2-3). Not a very pretty picture: God pumping the bellows on the blast furnace until our impurities are burned away.

Maybe we would prefer Isaiah.

"Comfort, comfort my people,"
    says your God.
"Speak tenderly to Jerusalem,
    and cry to her that her warfare
    is ended" (40:1-2a).

In a world whose economic, social, military and even religious joints often feel arthritic, how appropriate that word seems. "Comfort."

Among the most familiar--and best loved--snapshots of the Reign are the parables of Jesus. "With what can we compare the Reign of God . . . ? It is like a grain of mustard seed . . . . " (Mk. 4:30-32). The father and his two sons. The woman who stays up all night vacuuming the house until she finds her lost coin. And who doesn't get a little misty-eyed when Jesus lifts up a little child and says, "You must become like one of these" (Matt. 18:3).

But the author of Revelation hardly sees one who reminds him or her of a little child. "I saw one . . . like a son of man, clothed with a long robe and a golden girdle around his breast; his head and his hair were white as wool . . . his eyes were like a flame of fire, his feet were like burnished bronze, refined as in a furnace and his voice was like the sound of many waters . . . . " (1:12-16).

Why so many different snapshots? Perhaps because no one of them is enough to capture the breadth and depth and surprise of God's reign.

One of the most sensual images is a banquet. That may be what we have in the story of the feeding of the five thousand--a picture of what the reign of God is like: like a hungry crowd being fed in the wilderness.

Now that strikes me as odd. A banquet in the desert? After all, in the Bible the desert is frequently

115

a place forsaken by God. The only signs of life are a scorpion digging into a hole or a rock cracking under the sun. Waste we call it. Desert waste.

Now we are a long way from a desert. Even the Sand Hills are lush compared to real desert. But sometimes I feel like our world is forsaken by God. Nearly half the marriages I perform this year will end in divorce within five years. Our nuclear arsenal is big enough to kill every citizen of Russian fifty times, and the nuclear pistol Russia keeps in its holster is big enough to kill every one of us thirty times. And we talk about it as casually as we talk about the price of corn. Neither one is very encouraging. One of our shut-ins said to me this week, "Grand Island isn't safe anymore. I'd be afraid to go out at night. I think I'm going to buy a pistol and put it under my pillow." Right here in the All-American City. But I understand that feeling when I read about the young man who has no conscious recollection of robbing the Pump and Pantry and shooting a police officer in the leg.

We may not live in the land of baking rocks. But sometimes this world does feel like kind of a wilderness.

Yet the wilderness is just the place where God puts on the big feed. Perhaps that is because the wilderness is precisely the place where we need to know what the reign of God is like.

Now the setting is not the only thing that strikes me as odd about this banquet. Another is the main entree--bread and salted, dried fish.

I doubt that God is so unimaginative a cook that he can't think of anything else to fix. Some think that bread is intended to remind us of the bread-like substance called manna which God provided for the children of Israel when they were wandering in the wilderness for forty years. It got old, of course. Plain manna. Baked manna. Toasted manna. Fried manna. Manna frickasee. There are only so many things you can do with manna. But the point is that even in the wilderness, God provides.

But, there is a marked difference. In the wilderness for forty years, the children of Israel didn't have anything, and the manna came altogether as God's gracious gift. But the crowd with Jesus in the desert already has what God needs to prepare the banquet!

116

Bread and salted fish. This banquet doesn't require a French chef; it can take place with ordinary stuff--the kind of resources you and I have.

You see, God's banquet is not a middle class back yard bar-b-que. It celebrates those times when God takes the bread and fish out of our lunch pails and transforms at least a little piece of the wilderness into a place for celebration. It celebrates the victory of God over the injustice of the world. It celebrates making right the wrongs that people and cultures have suffered. It celebrates release from all kinds of oppression. It celebrates the end of poverty and the forgiveness of sin. It celebrates the day when the desert is overcome.

Isaiah puts it this way.

> The wilderness and dry land shall be glad,
>   the desert shall rejoice and blossom . . .
> Then the eyes of the blind shall be opened
>   and the ears of the deaf unstopped,
> then shall the lame leap like a deer
>   and the tongue of the dumb sing for joy.
>   (35:1, 6).

To be blind, deaf, lame, dumb is to live in a wilderness. To regain sight is reason for celebration.

The catch, of course, is that the banquet doesn't happen as long as we hold onto our bread and fish. The story of the feeding of the five thousand doesn't say exactly who had the food. But if he or she had kept it tucked under a robe or in a picnic basket, the crowd would probably have grumbled its way home. The miracle happens when we--you and I--offer our bread and fish, our ordinary stuff, to God.

So what do we have to offer? What are your bread and fish? A few minutes each day to make a phone call to check on a shut-in? Money for our denomination's Reconciliation program which will make loans to minority businesses? Two feet to march in a protest against the proliferation of nuclear arms--bread and fish which might save this whole planet from becoming a radioactive waste. The willpower to give up eating meat for just one day a week to help make grain available to someone starving on the Sahara desert--for whom a loaf of bread is, literally, a banquet?

117

I want you to notice something. All it took was
five loaves and two paltry fish, and God made plenty
of food for all. Now, I frequently hear people say,
"I just can't give up my bread and fish." "I don't
have the time." "Our church can't afford it just now--
the budget is too tight." "We're scared." "My loaves
are stale and my fish are guppies." But notice: in
this story God fills them all. And how much more full
those who brought the bread and fish--seeing how many
others were filled. I can hear them giving a sacramen-
tal burp.

I have seen it, bread and fish offered to God,
and overcoming at least a corner of the wilderness of
this world. Our congregation in Fort Collins, Colora-
do, discovered that some of its retired members did
not have enough income to pay the rent and to provide
a balanced diet. So as a congregation they are writing
monthly checks to help transform a little of this economic wilderness into fresh fruit and vegetables.

My friend Bob is in a wheelchair. He felt locked
out of many public buildings--including churches--until
ramps and other adjustments made it possible for him to
roll in. And where do I know him from? The YMCA
where such improvements have made it possible for him
to join the 500 Mile Swim Club. He swims only with
his arms. But it's possible because somebody offered
the bread and fish of their knowledge, time and money
so he can get in. You ought to hear him singing in the
shower. Well, on second thought, maybe you shouldn't.

In Zaire a few years ago, the average worker made
$ 75.00 a month. A month! And paid as much as $ 3.00
a pound for sugar and $ 6.00 a pound for meat. With no
money left for housing, most workers lived in mud huts
which degenerated in every rain. The thatch rocfs
were full of vermin and puddles on the dirt floors
were ideal mosquito-breeding grounds.

The Habitat for Humanity has for their motto, "A
decent house in a decent community for God's people in
need." Using little more than the bread and fish of
$ 2,000, a few piles of sand and the need for homes for
3,000 people, they have begun to build new housing
developments in Zaire.

Here is how Habitat's founder described the
dedication of one of their projects.

> At first there were hundreds of men
> and boys crowded around us, singing,
> shouting, dancing, clapping, praising
> the Lord. Then the number of people
> abruptly doubled as a great wave of
> women, singing in organized groups,
> came toward us. We moved very slowly
> because everyone wanted to shake hands,
> to shout a greeting, to point out
> something we simply must see. At one
> of the first spanking new houses we
> passed, the proud owner clutched me
> and jumped up and down again and again.
> He couldn't stop. He was absolutely
> beside himself with enthusiasm--he
> had a decent home![1]

A concrete slab. The kitchen is detached so it won't
smoke up the house. No plumbing. No electricity. Not
the whole answer. But a moment when the wilderness
gave way to celebration.

The story ends simply. "And they all ate and were
satisfied." I see them against the sunset, enjoying
the moment. Kids are throwing a frisbee. A man gives
a little belch and his wife looks at him in mild
shock. A woman lying on her back rubs her tummy and
stretches from top to toe.

But they cannot stay there. They go back through
the wilderness to their own homes and jobs. As long
as we live this side of the second coming, we can't
just sit around celebrating.

We go back to ironing long sleeve shirts and
punching the time clock and working geometry problems.
Ordinary stuff. Bread and fish. But that ordinary
stuff will never be quite the same because we know
what God can do with bread and fish. And who knows,
maybe God's reign will sneak up on us like it did one
day in the wilderness long ago, or maybe not so long
ago.

3. To Touch His Robe (Mark 5:25b-34)

Some stories have more to them than first meets
the ear. Take the story we read a few minutes ago.
It sounds like the simple story of a healing.

119

A woman has had a flow of blood for twelve years. Hard to know what the problem was; it could have been a skin ulcer, swollen and tight with a crater of pus and blood. Could have been a wound that refused to heal: the skin around the wound gets caked and hard but a raw crack in the middle is always oozing. Might have been a constant menstrual flow. Cramping and never dry.

You can imagine her state of mind. So desperate that she spent every dime she had going from clinic to clinic to clinic, only to watch the dripping grow into a trickle and the trickle into a stream.

Now she's in the sweaty, dusty crowd, her face half-covered by a veil. Her eyes. Can you see her eyes? Creased. Tense. Darting from face to face as she looks for the healer.

Maybe a cramp catches her as she bends, twisting and turning as she stretches her hand toward him. Hoping he doesn't shuffle out of reach, she stretches and strains the last inch and her fingers touch his robe, and she can feel the rough weave as her fingers brush by. And that night, for the first time in twelve years, she sleeps on a dry bed.

A healing story. But what does it have to do with me? I'm not a woman. I run six miles a day and the people at the bloodmobile say I have great blood. Dr. Cunningham tells me that a good coagulant would likely take care of a similar problem today. But there is more to the story than first meets the ear, and we may need an injection of background from the first century to hear it. Take these words from the book of Leviticus.

> When a woman has a prolonged discharge
> of blood for many days at a time other
> than her menstruation, her impurity shall
> last all the time of her discharge.
> She shall be unclean . . . Any bed on
> which she lies during the time of her
> discharge shall be like that which
> she used during menstruation and every-
> thing on which she sits shall be un-
> clean . . . Every person who touches
> them shall be unclean . . . . (15:25-27,
> passim).

Unclean. As long as she has the flow of blood, the
woman is unclean. That means religiously and socially
unacceptable. For twelve years this woman has lived
with the stigma of being unclean, treated like used
toilet paper.

She is cut off from the sacred places in the
temple and that is almost the same as cut off from
God. And she is cut off from other people. Wherever
she sits, wherever she walks, whatever she touches--
it's unclean. If she touches another person, that
person is unclean and must undergo a ritual process
for being restored to cleanliness. She is like the
West Point Cadets who reported the cheating scandal.
Shunned. She received the same welcome as the draft
resistors who appeared at the convention of the
Veterans of Foreign Wars on the same day that convention passed a resolution declaring the pardoning of
such resistors a "Day of Infamy."

Now to me it seems irrational for a person to be
treated that way because of a little blood. It seems
even crazier, even inhumane, that just when she needed
love and care, she found herself fenced off from those
who could give it to her. But rational or not, her
experience is real.

Have you ever had that experience--finding the
world pulling away from you as though you were contagious? Do you know someone who has?

With divorce papers in hand, a woman realizes that
"divorce" is spelled "quaratined" to many of her
friends. They don't know what to say or do. Perhaps
unconsciously, they think, "If it could happen to her,
maybe it could happen to me." And so the phone is
quiet.

Not long ago a man who lost his wife to death
asked me about a couple he and his wife used to run
around with. "How are they doing these days?" In fact
he wondered what had become of a lot of his friends who
were still together. How many times have I heard
single people say they feel like a "third wheel?"

I do not know how many of our members who live
in nursing homes have said, in one way or another,
"I just wish I could die. The world is finished with
me and I'm no earthly good." They feel like dirty
linen with no way to be washed.

We have a friend graduating near the top of the class in seminary. President of the student body. Assistant to the dean. Soon to be ordained. But feeling unwanted because <u>she</u> has yet to have a decent interview with a church.

In Southern Missouri, I was in the second grade when the public schools integrated, and I remember a girl from our class telling a bunch of us on the corner of the playground that if we touched a black person-- and that wasn't the word she used--the black would rub off on us. Is it any wonder blacks were systematically sealed out of the mainstream of American life?

Is the story of the woman with the flow of blood strictly the story of a physical problem? No. So when the woman found healing, she found that the end of the flow of blood opened the chain-link fence around her life. She was free to go. As with wire cutters, the social stigma was cut. Today we might say that the social structure which kept her repressed was broken.

But it didn't just happen. She wasn't healed simply by wishing to be whole. She had to push through the sweaty crowd to touch his robe. And the point is not so much the robe, but that when she touched it she placed herself in the sphere of God's healing power and influence. When she came into contact with that sphere it changed the conditions of her life. She felt like she had just stepped out of the shower.

We do not have that physical robe to touch. Those who told and heard this story after the resurrection did not have that physical presence either. But because of the resurrection, they found that same power at work when they saw an unclean woman feeling clean, an unacceptable man feeling acceptable.

What do you think? Do we experience that power the same way--whenever those declared unclean and unacceptable discover that that those labels no longer apply to them? It sometimes happens in a change in attitude and it sometimes happens in a change of the conditions of life.

Jesus said to her, "Your faith has made you well." In the case of this woman, faith is the trust to put herself in such a place that the healing power could influence her. She had to give God room to work. And sometimes that's what faith is--making yourself

122

open to people, places and power which can stop the flow of blood.

Now if Jesus is still resurrected, then whenever and wherever people are restored to wholeness of life, God's power is at work. Whenever someone feeling unclean and unacceptable begins to feel clean and accepted, God's power is at work. In faith, we get close enough to that power so that it can work.

One of my early-morning running buddies is Hispanic. As we gasped around on the track not long ago, he told me about growing up as a migrant. Always treated as temporary. On the edge--but never at the center--of things. Not allowed to date girls who lived in town. Living on borrowed money from camp to camp. Without legal protection. A scholarship enabled him to leave the migrant life. "My feeling about myself changed. I felt like a whole new person." And I heard that power at work when he said, "I realize we need more than scholarships. We need to change the way migrants live, the way they are treated by this society."

I heard that power at a recent meeting when a man stood up for the first time and said, "I'm Bill and I'm an alchoholic." The battle isn't over, but in AA he has found a healing community.

THEOS has given our widows and widowers a place where they feel like they belong. "I never feel embarrassed to cry here."

A call came late at night. "Can you come over?" I had been suspicious about her almost from the first time I had preached in that small summer church. Young. Attractive. Bubbly. Just divorced.

John Denver was singing softly on the stereo. The lamplight was gentle. A scented candle was burning. As we talked, her concerns did not seem urgent, and I thought my suspicions were confirmed.

Perhaps something communicated itself because she asked, "You look like you're sitting on eggs. How come?" A long, awkward silence. "What kind of woman do you think I am?"

It was quiet as midnight. She buried her face in her hands and her whole body shook. "Oh God, I feel so . . . unclean." Guilt about the divorce. Lectures

123

from her family. Her boss had asked her to go on a
low-budget trip, so low that they would need to share a
room. Her last date had been all hands. And now, her
minister.

As we talked, a theme emerged. The place where
she had found relationships that were healing and
honest was that struggling, small church. The people
had, literally, put their arms around her and held her.
They had not asked nosey questions. They even invited
her to join the choir.

"Ron, there were times when that bunch of people
was all that kept me going. I don't know what I would
have done without them. I just seemed to belong."

Call it a neat little preacher's story if you
want. But I hear in her what I heard in the story of
a woman who lived twenty centuries before.

NOTES

[1]Millard Fuller and Diane Scott, Love in the Mor-
tar Joints (Chicago: Association, 1980), p. 22.

BASIC BIBLIOGRAPHY ON THE MIRACLE STORIES

This is a bibliography of general and basic works on the miracle stories. Articles dealing with specific passages and questions may be easily located in the standard bibliographies. Entries marked with an asterisk (*) would prove useful in a pastor's library.

Achtemeier, Paul J. "Gospel Miracle Tradition and the Divine Man." Interp 26 (1972), pp. 174-97.

_____. "Toward the Isolation of Pre-Markan Miracle Catenae." JBL 89 (1970), pp. 265-91.

_____. "The Origin and Function of the Pre-Markan Miracle Catenae." JBL 91 (1972), pp. 198-221.

_____. "The Lukan Perspective on the Miracles of Jesus: A Preliminary Sketch." Perspectives on Luke-Acts. Ed. Charles Talbert. Edinburgh: T & T Clark, 1978, pp. 153- 167. Also in JBL 94 (1975), pp. 471-91.

Baltensweiter, H. "Wunder und Glaube im Neuen Testament." TZ 23 (1967), pp. 24-56.

*Bartlett, David L. Fact and Faith. Valley Forge: Judson, 1975.

Becker, Juergen. "Wunder und Christologie." NTS 16 (1969-70), pp. 130-48.

Betz, Hans Dieter. "Jesus as Divine Man." Jesus and the Historian. Ed. F.T. Trotter. Philadelphia: Westminster, 1968, pp. 113-133.

Bieler, Ludwig. Theios Aner, Das Bild des "Goettlichen Menschen" in Spaetantike under Fruechristentum, 2 vols. Wien: Hoefels, 1935-6.

Bonner, Campbell. "Traces of Thaumaturgic Technique in the Miracles." Harvard Theological Review 20 (1927), pp. 271-81.

_____. "The Technique of Exorcism." Harvard Theological Review 36 (1943), pp. 39-49.

*Bornkamm, Guenther. G. Barth and H.J. Held. Tradition and Interpretation in Matthew. Tr. P. Scott. Philadelphia: Westminster, 1963.

Brown, Raymond. "The Gospel Miracles." New Testament Studies. Ed. J. McKenzie. Milwaukee: Bruce, 1965, pp. 168-191.

*Bultmann, Rudolf. The History of the Synoptic Tradition. Tr. J. Marsh. London: Blackwell, 1963, pp. 209-243.

Case, Shirley J. Experience with the Supernatural in Early Christian Times. New York: Century, 1929.

_____. "The Art of Healing in Early Christian Times." Journal of Religion 3 (1923), pp. 238-55.

Delling, Gerhard. "Zur Beusteilung des Wunder durch Antike." Wissenschaftliche Zeitschrift der Ernst-Maritz-Arndt Universitaet Griefswald 5 (1955-56), pp. 221-229.

_____. Antike Wundertexte. Berlin: de Gruyter, 1960.

_____. "Das Verstandnis des Wunder im Neuen Testament." Zeitschrift fuer systematische Theologie 24 (1955), pp. 265-80.

*Dibelius, Martin. From Tradition to Gospel. Tr. B. Woolf. New York: Charles Scribner's Sons, 1934, pp. 70-104.

Fiebig, Paul. Antike Wundergeschichten. Bonn: Marcus and Weber, 1911.

_____. Juedische Wundergeschichten des neutestamentlichen Zeitalters. Tuebingen: J.C.B. Mohr, 1911.

*Fridrichsen, Anton. The Problem of Miracle in Primitive Christianity. Tr. R. Harrisville and J. Hanson. Minneapolis: Augsburg, 1972.

*Fuller, R.H. Interpreting the Miracles. London: SCM, 1963.

Grant, Robert M. Miracle and Natural-Law in Graeco-Roman and Early Christian Thought. Amsterdam: North Holland, 1952.

Gutbrod, Karl. Die Wundergeschichten des Neuen Testaments. Stuttgart: Calwer, 1968.

Hempel, Johannes. Heilung als Symbol und Wirklichkeit im biblischen Schriftum. Goettingen: Vandenhoeck and Ruprecht, 1965.

Hiers, Richard. "Satan, Demons and the Kingdom of God." SJT 27 (1974), pp. 35-47.

Hull, John M. Hellenistic Magic and the Synoptic Tradition. SBT Second Series 28. Naperville: Allenson, 1974.

Kaesemann, Ernst. "Wunder im Neuen Testament." RGG3 Vol. VI, p. 1836.

Kee, Howard C. "The Terminology of Mark's Exorcism Stories." NTS 14 (1968), pp. 131-149.

*Keller, Ernst and Marie-Luise Keller. Miracles in Dispute. Tr. M. Kohl. Philadelphia: Fortress, 1969.

Kertelege, Karl. Die Wunder Jesu im Markusevangelium. Munich: Koesel, 1970.

*Lewis, C.S. Miracles. London: Fontana, 1960.

McCasland, S.V. By the Finger of God. New York: Macmillan, 1951.

_____. "Religious Healing in First Century Palestine." Environmental Factors in Christian History. Ed. J. McNeill, et. al. Chicago: Univeristy of Chicago, 1939, pp. 18-34.

_____. "Signs and Wonders." JBL 76 (1957), pp. 149-52.

127

McGinley, Laurence J. _Form-Criticism of the Synoptic Healing Narratives_. Woodstock, Md.: Woodstock College Press, 1944.

Moulse, C.F.D., ed. _Miracles_. London: Mowbray, 1965.

Parker, Pierson. "Early Christianity as a Religion of Healing." _St. Luke's Journal of Theology_ 19 (1976), pp. 142-150.

Perels, Otto. _Die Wunderuberlieferung der Synoptiker_. Berlin: Stuttgart: Kohlhammer, 1934.

Renner, Rudolf. _Die Wunder Jesu_. Lahr-Schwarzwald: Marits Schauenberg, 1966.

Richardson, Alan. _The Miracle Stories of the Gospels_. London: SCM, 1941.

Sabourin, L. "Miracles of Jesus: Preliminary Survey." _Biblical Theology Bulletin_ 1 (1971), pp. 59-80.

_____. "Miracles of Jesus: Jesus and the Evil Powers." _Biblical Theology Bulletin_ 4 (1974), pp. 115-175.

_____. "Miracles of Jesus: Healings, Resuscitations and Nature Miracles." _Biblical Theology Bulletin_ 5 (1975), pp. 159-72.

Schamoni, W. _Paralleln zum Neuen Testament aus Heilungsprechungssachten uebersetz_. Abensberg: Kral, 1971.

Schenke, Ludger. _Die Wunderzaehlungen des Markusevangeliums_. Stuttgart: Katholisches Bibelwerk, 1974.

Schille, G. _Die Urchristliche Wundertradition_. Stuttgart: Calwer, 1967.

Schlingensiepen, Herman. _Die Wunder des Neuen Testaments_. Guetersloh: Bertelsmann, 1933.

*_Semeia_ 11 (1978).

Tagawa, Kenzo. _Miracles et Évangile: Le Pensée personnelle de l'évangéliste Marc_. Paris: Presses Universitaires de France, 1966.

Theissen, Gerd. Urchristliche Wundergeschichten.
Guetersloh: Gerd Mohn, 1974.

Van der Loos, H. The Miracles of Jesus. Leiden:
Brill, 1975.

Weinrich, Otto. Antike Heilungswunder. Giessen:
Toepelmann, 1911.